Why It's OK to Talk to Your Dog

Co-evolution of People and Dogs

David Paxton

First published in 2011.

National Library of Australia Cataloguing-in-Publication entry:

Author:	Paxton, David.
Title:	Why it's ok to talk to your dog / David Paxton.
ISBN:	9781921555787 (pbk.)
eISBN:	9781921555923 (pbk.)
Subjects:	Dogs.
	Human-animal relationships.
	Animals and civilization.

Dewey Number: 636.7

Typeset in Serifa

Published by David W. Paxton

Printed and bound by Watson Ferguson & Company, Salisbury, Brisbane, Australia.

Illustrations by Samantha Paxton www.cheekychoppy.com

Front cover design by Andrew Paxton; chalk and charcoal painting Hugo Erfurth with Ajax (1926) by Otto Dix, German master painter, copyright Bild-Kunst/Viscopy (Australia); photoimage credit bpk/ Kupferstichkabinett, SMB/ Jörg P. Anders

www.compositeconversationalist.com

For John Alan Corrigan
(14.11.1904 – 3.2.1986)
and
Marguerite Vivienne Corrigan
(11.9.1897 – 30.5.1987),
and my father,
David Anthony Paxton
(25.4.1917 – 2.7.1974).

Acknowledgements

It is a pleasure to acknowledge the help I received from Lisa Beck. She is a good correspondent with sound academic judgment. I learnt a lot from her.

Alan and Vivienne Corrigan were my guardians and left me a legacy in the late 1980s, which assisted me to educate all the family and return to university myself, aided by scholarships from the Australian Government and the Australian National University.

Others who helped me include Shannon Ryan, Margie Riley, Margaret Saunders, Norma Green, John Auty, Margaret Boland, Peter and Ronnie Ross, and Norah Allan (who all read drafts and commented); Dorothy Boland (my late mother-in-law) who always thought the idea of the book was rather smart and whose Latin group helped create one of the chapter headings; Stephen Ross with his sage legal advice; staff at Boolarong Press; Lesley Rogers and Gisela Kaplan gave helpful advice on producing the book, and I apologise to Lesley again for smashing one of her fine teacups as I gestured excitedly while explaining my idea.

Personal friends Megan and Phillip Wallens, Beverley and Brian Pearce, Pamela and Lyall McEwin, Jennifer and Brian Wood, John and Deidre Christie, Colin Collins and Diane Gillham all provided encouragement and moral support.

My immediate family was very much involved. My wife Ellen Paxton and daughters Belinda and Gillian offered opinions which helped form the structure of the book. My admirable daughter Samantha drew the diagrams with enviable skill; and my talented son Andrew designed the cover.

Taj Books International, Surrey kindly permitted the use of diagrams from *Human Anatomy*. Charles C. Thomas, Illinois permitted use of diagrams from *Evolution of the Speech Apparatus*. The Natural

History Museum, London permitted use of photographs of *Homo* skulls. Pearson Education, Harlow had no objection to the use of diagrams from *Topographical Anatomy of the Dog*. The original art work in those books was used to inform explanatory diagrams in this book.

Financial assistance to help prepare the book for publication was received from the Regional Arts Development Fund, which is a Queensland Government and Redland City Council partnership to support local arts and culture.

DWP

Contents

Illustrations

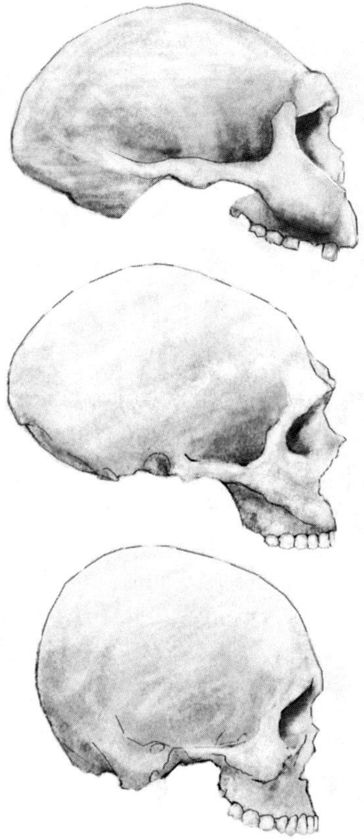

***Homo erectus* skull**
Homo erectus lived from about 2 million years ago to about 200,000 years ago.

***Homo neanderthalensis* skull**
Homo neanderthalensis lived from about 400,000 years ago to about 30,000 years ago.

***Homo sapiens* skull**
Homo sapiens has lived since about 130,000 years ago.

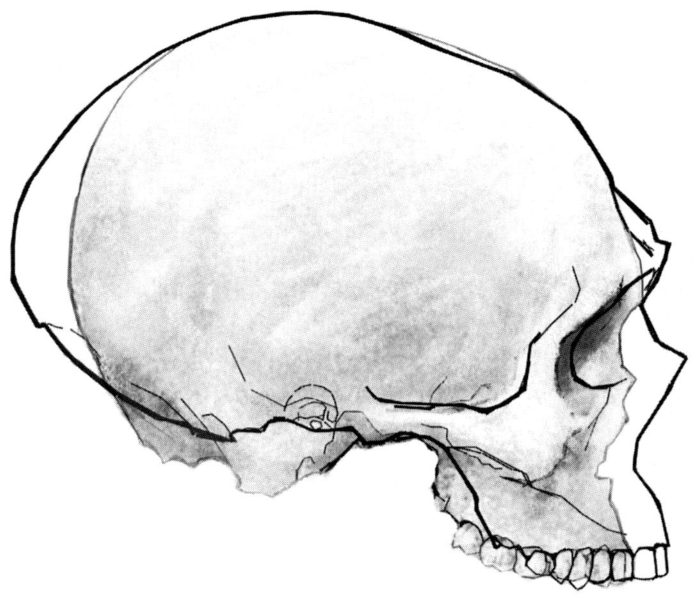

When *H. neanderthalensis* and *H. sapiens* skulls are overlaid, the significant difference in facial proportions is evident.

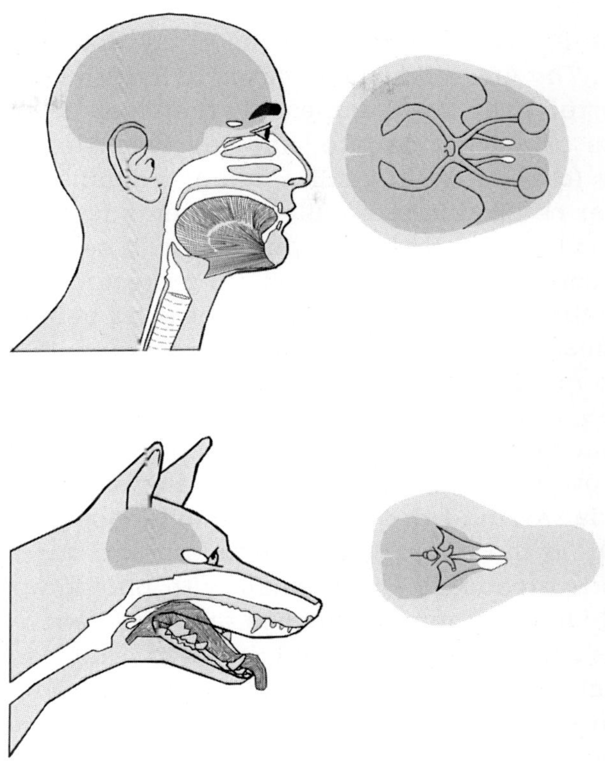

Human anatomy for speech compared with canine anatomy for smelling and catching prey. Note that the human olfactory membranes are reduced, the tongue acts as a relatively controlled piston and the entrance to the trachea (windpipe) faces back to the spinal column and into pharynx. Note also the efficient alignment of the dog's catching, smelling, gulping and swallowing, and breathing apparatuses.

The base of the human brain (top) shows great evolvement of the cerebral hemispheres. The olfactory bulbs, the two structures lying inside the optic nerves leading from the eyeballs, are relatively much reduced. In comparison, the base of the dog brain (below) shows massive evolvement of olfactory bulbs and relatively small evolvement of cerebral hemispheres In the diagram of the dog brain, the eyeballs and connecting optic nerves are not shown.

Preface

While I was writing one of the many drafts of this book, *The Australian* newspaper (10 September 2010) reported that the European Parliament, after two years of heated debate, had resolved that Great Apes (chimpanzees, gorillas and orangutans) will no longer be used in stressful experiments for scientific research, and use of other primates will be curtailed. The conservatives in the debate protested that the resolution went too far: an animal is an animal and a human being is a human being, two quite different matters. Two weeks before, in its weekend edition (28-29 August 2010), the same paper reported that an Iranian Grand Ayatollah had moved a fatwa against dog ownership, stating that dogs are unclean under Sharia law and dog-keeping is evidence of moral decay in the urban elites. A month ago one of my friends broadcast a joke email with photographs of the billboards of two churches that faced each other across a street in the United States of America. One church advertised that dogs of its parishioners could go to Heaven; the other responded that dogs do not have souls and therefore could not go to Heaven. The exchange escalated in an amusing way until pet rocks became the subjects of contention.

Views on the natural world can thus be quite divergent and I have written this book to broaden the discussion further, by dealing with human beings and dogs as animals that co-evolved. In other words, people and dogs are animals in a natural relationship; they are part of each other's nature. For those who do not accept that the human being is an animal, this will seem a radical proposition. For others who do accept that human beings are animals, linking their evolution with that of the dog may also seem radical. I ask the reader to consider that our relationship with dogs does have natural ramifications and therefore a naturalistic perspective is desirable.

Most people who read this book will live in urban situations and will be aware of the dog as an animal whose keeping is regulated by local governments. The dog is a perennial source of conflict in the communities that local governments hope to govern with a minimum of fuss. I think dogs are a natural part of a healthy community and need to be managed positively. Prohibitions on dog keeping are unnatural and will ultimately be unjust and counterproductive.

Public policy on the urban dog is often stated briefly as "responsible dog ownership". In practice, this can become a way of defining "irresponsible" minorities in society rather than developing reasonable policy. "Ownership" of animals is a thought construct that many keepers of animals do not accept. The statement reveals an attitude that needs to be moderated by an appreciation of the dog as a natural and necessary part of a vibrant human society. The statement objectifies the dog and the dog-keeper. Since the relationship is natural and evolved, it actually is subjective. A naturalistic discourse is an alternative view that is not value-laden and so can lead to better governance.

Another reason I have written this book is to make my point of view accessible in detail for the first time. I first published the broad idea in 1994 and, over the years since, a number of writers have referred to it with varying accuracy. One cited my idea in support of werewolves, attributing to me the idea that dogs somehow created people. I hope this book will clear up any misunderstandings on that score.

My basic degree is in veterinary science, but a wonderful opportunity arose to accept scholarships to study in political science and international relations as a mature-age student at the Australian National

University in Canberra, Australia in 1992. I chose public policy on urban dogs as a case study. In 1994 I presented a paper at an urban animal management conference convened by the Australian Veterinary Association. That paper attracted media interest, including attention from Jonica Newby, a young veterinarian embarking on a career in radio and television journalism.

Jonica Newby wrote *The Pact for Survival,* published in 1997. That book was later renamed *Animal Attraction*. She dedicated the book to me and, in the early part of the book, discussed my idea. *The Pact for Survival* was noted by a British documentary filmmaker, David Paterson. By this time, I was leading an Australian aid project in Papua New Guinea. David visited Port Moresby with a team, I took leave, and we recorded a significant amount of film footage and audio tape for his film called *The Secret Life of the Dog*, which he produced for BBC Channel 4 and the Discovery Channel. The film was released in 1998.

My doctorate was awarded in 1999 and in 2000 the International Society for Anthrozoology published a commentary on my perspective in its journal, *Anthrozoös.* In 2003 the Society kindly allowed me to give a paper entitled *Why It's OK to Talk to Your Dog* at its annual conference, held that year at Kent State University, Akron, Ohio. The Petcare Information and Advisory Service in Australia paid my airfares.

Lisa Beck, a social psychologist at Bryn Mawr University in Philadelphia, contacted me in 2007. Lisa taught a course on exploring animal minds. We began to correspond. Lisa had access to the latest research publications so our correspondence was of great benefit to me. We decided to write a book together, me to write on the naturalistic perspective and Lisa to write on its social and psychological implications. When the time came for semi-final drafting and for juggling real lives and priorities, however, it soon became clear that writing a cohesive text and finding a publisher would be difficult. Lisa decided to concentrate on another research interest and her family, but encouraged me to persevere with a shorter, more focused book.

This is that book. Its theme is unorthodox and necessarily speculative. This, I think, is preferable to the non-speculative orthodox view that dogs are created, owned objects.

At the end of the book is a list of most of the books, papers and other visual media that I found interesting. Authors referred to in the text can be found in that list.

Chapter One - Introducing an Idea

Those who dare to be aware,
Those who think outside the square,
Those who seldom are dead sure,
They are thought rich, belief poor.

The ancestors of the dog were an integral, essential part of the evolution of human beings. Our ancestors were an integral, essential part of the evolution of dogs. Dogs and people are part of each other's biology. To deny this is to deny our own biological natures. That, in a nutshell, is what this book is about.

We take ourselves and our relationship with dogs pretty much for granted, but, if we think critically, it is clear that we are so strange, and our relationship with dogs is so strange, that there are many questions which beg to be asked.

Why is the attachment between us and dogs so firm? Why so enduring and so deep? Why do we engage with each other so well that we call the dog our best friend? And why does that friendship spread so wide, between cultures and geographies, between age groups and genders?

We take puppies into our homes and tolerate them piddling, puking and pooing. We clean up after them. We forgive them for chewing our cherished possessions. Our hearts melt at their cuteness, their warmth and exuberance, their apparent ability to read our moods. As the puppies grow we become their willing stewards, providing sustenance, shelter and affection. As they age we sympathise with them for their aches and pains, adjust our expectations of them, and grieve when they die.

Our dog is part of the family even when, perhaps especially when, that family is only a "Pack of Two", the title of Caroline Knapp's book on the intricate relationship between urban people and dogs. The family structure adjusts to accommodate the dog, its meal times, walk times, sleep times and play times. Young children, growing adults and mature adults as well find that the dog is often the only constant in a demanding and conflicted world, a companion upon whom they can rely for non-judgmental affection.

Why, for us, is the dog a window into a world of smells and sounds we can appreciate no other way? Why is it a delight to take the dog for a walk, and why does it warn us of dangers? Why does the dog help us live in the moment, when our own tendency is towards caution? Why, when I take our dog Toby to visit my mother at her retirement village, is he mobbed (in slow motion) like a rock star by people who want to pat him?

Why does the dog seem to be beneficial to our health and wellbeing, according to quantitative and qualitative studies? Why can it aid hearing- and vision-impaired people, and those subject to seizures? Why does the dog enhance security of our persons, our property and our armed services in ways that modern technology cannot practically achieve? In a nutshell, why is the dog so doggone useful? This quality cannot be dismissed as acquired through the guidance of human dog breeders and trainers, because no other animal is so generally integrated with human endeavour.

In affluent societies some people may appear to have a one-dimensional relationship with dogs, they may appear to regard them as simply status symbols or fashion accessories, but the relationship still has complexity. After all, a diamond bracelet or expensive wrist-watch might make the same statement about the wearer, but would be easier to keep than a dog, and perhaps less expensive overall. In less affluent societies, where the dog is not managed, the village dogs may appear to be in a loose relationship with the human community, but appearances can be misleading – an enduring relationship is there; the dog is an inevitable part of the human landscape. Although only some dogs may wear a collar or other mark of belonging to someone, the community is aware of all of them and aware of the complex relationship between the people and dogs in that community.

The poorest of the poor, living in the streets and squatter settlements of cities around the world, engage with dogs even though they have so few resources for themselves. In a suburb of Jaipur in India, a small boy in tattered clothes held up a puppy for me to care for; the boy's head crawled so thickly with lice that they were easily visible to me as I leant down to take the pup from him. But his concern was for the tiny, skinny pup. In Madras, another Indian city, in a street near the bus station, people lived under frayed tent-like structures. Their only water supply seemed to be the grey puddles in the gutter. I saw a woman hold a young dog up to her cheek in a clear gesture of affection. The futures for the woman and for the dog must have been very bleak, yet they responded to each other.

Why would that young dog allow itself to be held, cheek-to-cheek, by another species? Dogs allow us to house-train them to the point that a healthy dog would "die" of embarrassment rather than soil itself or the house; obedience train them; collar, lead, fence, cuddle and kiss them. Dogs generally accept a relationship with us that other animals would find confronting if not intolerable. Why does the dog not return to the wild like a noble savage?

The answer to all the above questions is that there is a bond between people and dogs that is insoluble. Explanations for the bond may include social, economic and psychological reasons. The answer this book puts forward is that the human-dog bond is elemental, an evolved, natural, biological phenomenon. We need the dog because it is part of our own evolution.

Anywhere there are people there are dogs. The relationship is unequivocal, ubiquitous, universal and unique. The biology of people and dogs is interdependent. Dependency lies deep in the heart of both our natures.

So, this book is about two animals, *Homo sapiens* and *Canis familiaris*, and their ancestors. Among all those ancestors, human beings stand out as being very odd. Indeed we are the only ones left standing of an array of past *Homo* species. The dog is pretty odd too, when compared in its enormous variety of form with the wolves that exist so tenuously today.

The enduring close relationship between the dog and us is yet another of those oddities. There is no other relationship like it in the animal world. This book speculates on our co-evolution with the dog since 130,000 years or so ago. It does not ignore the 90 per cent of human and canine existence that books on people and dogs usually do. It gives the dog natural rather than derived status, and treats people the same way. It argues that people and dogs have been blended by the process of natural selection.

The story is organised by the theory of natural selection. That theory underpins biology, so this story is actually a hypothesis, which I have named the Composite Conversationalist Hypothesis, because my argument is that we and dogs together make up a composite animal that has the ability to speak.

Anthropomorphism can be good

We are being anthropomorphic when we attribute human qualities to an(other) animal. This can be criticised: We are sentimentally muddying the waters of sane discussion about the natural world, which we might consider at best to be in our stewardship or, at worst, an oyster to pry open and guzzle. However, Charles Darwin forced us to consider ourselves as animals and to reconsider our relationship with nature. The Composite Conversationalist Hypothesis is that people and dogs are natural extensions of each other, we are blended in some way, and so a good deal of anthropomorphic attribution seems to me to be quite all right.

Within a family, people talk to the dog because he or she is a member of the family. I have already mentioned our dog, Toby. He is perhaps a German Shepherd crossbred with the possibility of some dingo genes. Toby was born in Cairns, North Queensland. There, when young, he was kicked by a cassowary bird and still bears the scar. Cassowaries are armed with lethal claws on their feet. Toby has been on the lookout for cassowaries ever since and any loud noise, cutlery clattering in the sink, say, causes him to leap up and skitter for safety, sizeable though he is. Startled, we then exclaim, "For goodness sake, Toby!"

and Toby looks shamefaced and hard done by, before returning to his nap.

Toby is a sociable dog who really likes people. He came to us when a niece and her family moved to the city. She was concerned that he might be run over by a car. We live on a small island so there is less chance of that happening. Many people talk to Toby. I might say, "Good morning, Toby" and ruffle his fur. If I'm feeling good, I might exclaim, "G'day, Furry One!" and Toby will bound and do a little dance, although his joints now creak lamentably. My family and close friends speak to Toby as though he were a person. My mother-in-law Dorothy used to say, "Toby, you have a good life" and thus infer that all was well with the household. My wife Ellen might say, "Toby, you're getting fat!" – and dart an accusing look at me (Ellen comments: "Now you're being paranoid. But you *do* spoil Toby!"). Friends might say "Are they treating you well, Toby?" Toby seems to be taking all this in, because he responds appropriately, with a smile and a wag of his tail or he stoops and his ears droop. An animal behaviourist might say that Toby is merely showing appeasement[1] behaviour, but we prefer to think he knows that we are communicating with him.

Our wonderful neighbour, Margaret, recently widowed, has taken Toby for a walk, rain or shine, every morning for about six years. She definitely thinks he is an individual with many human qualities. Her husband, Brian, used to call Toby "Master Paxton" and say that Toby should be Prime Minister one day, because he was so good at getting his own way.

1. One night in March 2011 I was called to see a nine year old Fox Terrier who had bitten a cane toad (*Bufo marinus*). These toads exude a poison from glands behind their ears which is bitter and toxic. The dog was paralysed rigid, was hyperventilating and its blood pressure, as shown by its brick red gums, was very high. I had known this friendly little dog for years. She seemed to recognise me and *tried to wag her tail*. Hardly appeasement behaviour, I think. The dog recovered in a few hours, thanks to good nursing by her two keepers.

Generally though, when with strangers and acquaintances, we talk about our dog, not directly to him or her. We are shy about sentimentality. I find this intriguing. In private the dog is the subject of conversation, in public it is the object of conversation.

This alternating subject/objectivity is perhaps reflective of our ambivalent attitude to animals generally. The magic of subjectivity is pressured by theological premises of the separateness of human beings from nature and also by economic and scientific objectivity. There is a long history explaining these pressures. An example is the lasting influence of Saint Thomas Aquinas (1225 – 1274), the Roman Catholic Church's philosopher, who considered that only human beings had godly essence (souls) and so were separate from Nature, which merely existed. A more modern example is the effect of René Descartes' (1596 – 1650) publication of his method for achieving scientific rigor by the meticulous collection of facts, which still influences the prevailing world view, in the West at least, even though he kept one prudent eye on the Inquisition as he wrote. His philosophy differentiated human beings, who could think and hence *were*, from animals, who could not think (he thought) and hence *weren't* – they simply were machines: automations. Descartes' scientific method shaped scientific views powerfully and productively, but to the detriment of appreciating animals as sentient beings. It also affronted people who felt a kinship with animals, such as his contemporary, the English philosopher Henry More, who accused him of murderous arrogance. René Descartes was unabashed, arguing that his philosophy was "indulgent to men" and convenient to human interests (see Richard Ryder). This is a rather canny appraisal of human attitudes to animals in general, but many modern philosophers have recoiled from Descartes' philosophy. The list is long, but two in particular influenced my thinking. Mary Midgley stated that the question we should ask is what distinguishes people *among* the animals, not what distinguishes people *from* animals, and Barbara Noske argued that public policy is necessarily flawed unless decision-makers regard animals as the subject of policy, not merely as objects.

Official discourse may necessarily be centred on the human being – anthropocentric – because it is about the disposition of resources for human benefit. However, anthropocentricism needs to be leavened by other perspectives, such as moral, ethical and naturalistic perspectives. We are one animal among many others. Their evolution is as unique as ours is. We are not separate from them. Among the many meanings of what it is to be human, one is that we are part of an evolving complex of animals within which the dog is particularly significant. Anthropocentricism may be an explanation for the way we view this world, but it is not an excuse for condemning anthropomorphism out of hand, especially in relation to the dog.

It is perfectly OK to talk to your dog. You need not be shy about it in public because you would not be able to enunciate clearly if it were not for the dog. You might not exist at all except for the dog. Without the dog there might not be *Homo sapiens*, the Wise Man, who talks, and writes and reads.

Words maketh the wo/man

Words are only possible because we have the anatomy for speech, that is, the anatomy to utter clipped intelligible words strung in sentences, and the cerebral anatomy to make up, perceive and understand those words. From words we can build complicated messages and mind-blowing concepts and magical symbols. Clear diction requires an appropriate anatomy of the chest, larynx (voice-box), throat, mouth and face. This will be discussed later in some detail, particularly the anatomy of the head, in relation to our co-evolution with the dog. Appropriate anatomy, of the brain in particular, is necessary to conceive words and to understand words. There will be brief discussion of this as well, in relation to language. The anatomy for speech evolved and persisted because it was one of many physical characteristics that helped our species to compete, adapt and survive alongside other similar *Homo* species in our immediate environment. Those other *Homo* species could communicate with each other, they had language, but they could not communicate quite as well as we could. The word was the beginning for us, but the end for them.

This is a very simple statement, but it is possible only because of the illuminative genius of Charles Darwin and Alfred Russel Wallace, who first stated it intelligibly in 1858 when they surveyed current knowledge on evolution and theorised that species originated by means of natural selection.

Our species is the only one that can manipulate words to convey complex information accurately. This information can be used, shared and built on by others, and then be shared again. This capability is enormously powerful for the survival of our species, which, by most physical standards, is not particularly impressive. Ironically, the anatomy that has evolved and made speech possible was also non-adaptive for survival in other ways. The irony is discussed briefly below, but the anatomy will be discussed in greater detail later.

Our large brain dictates the need for a large, heavy head, which has to be supported from directly underneath by our neck, to balance its considerable weight. In other mammals, the neck attaches further back in the head. Their heads are more in line with the horizontal axis of their bodies. Because of the rotated head, arguably, our faces have "fallen" and are quite flat. We have no muzzle, unlike other mammals. It is important to realise this. Our nose may appear pronounced, but it really consists only of two tubes or nostrils containing a few unsightly hairs. You can check that this is so by looking with a mirror and a torch. Our smelling apparatus (the nasal mucosa) actually is inside the skull, under our eyes, and consists of a meagre area of nasal membrane mounted on soft bones or cartilage. When you peered up your nostrils, you may have detected just a pink hint of the apparatus.

We have a poor sense of smell, yet a good sense of smell is of primary importance for the survival of other terrestrial mammals. Indeed, the ability to smell was among the earliest sensations to evolve. The olfactory bulbs in our brains are small in comparison with those of the dog. A dog's nasal membranes are relatively huge, and its sense of smell is phenomenal in comparison with ours.

The rotated head and flat face in people creates a small bite that aids clear diction, but also creates a situation in which the widest part of the baby's head is presented at the moment of birth. Death in childbirth is a very common risk for human beings. Human mothers run a much greater risk of dying when giving birth than other mammalian mothers whose infants have proportionally narrow heads. The evolution of difficult birth seems an oxymoronic flight in the face of logic.

A small bite in human beings is great for proper enunciation. Our tongue does not loll as it does in the muzzle of a panting dog, but has reduced in length to work as a piston, better for pumping out sounds. The reduction in the size of our upper and lower jawbones may leave insufficient room for wisdom teeth to descend normally into the line of teeth in the jaws. They become displaced or impacted and can seriously affect health and wellbeing. Young modern human adults suffer migraine headaches because of impacted wisdom teeth, which thus require orthodontic intervention.

Because we are bipedal and walk upright, and our head has rotated, our larynx (the voice-box or Adam's apple) drops and hangs backward, due to the pull of gravity. This gives us an enlarged voice chamber for making the sounds of speech, but reverses our epiglottis (the valve that prevents food entering the windpipe) such that it turns almost completely to face back, instead of forward into the airway from the nose as it does in other mammals. Instead it faces into the chamber where the esophagus or food passage has its opening. This is why food or drink so easily "goes down the wrong way" in human beings and triggers the epiglottis into spasm, making us choke. Choking is a very unpleasant sensation, as King Henry I of England found to his mortification, when he choked to death on a surfeit of lampreys. Choking remains a common reality of the human condition.

How did we evolve in this way? We appear to be out of step with the process of natural selection. Indeed, despite co-inventing the explanation for biological evolution, Alfred Russel Wallace actually came to think that the frailties of human beings perhaps might be proof that we were not subject to natural selection after all.

But we did become a species through a process of natural selection, like any other species. Our frailties were outweighed by our capacity for enunciated speech, which gave us an overwhelming advantage over competing species in the struggle for existence. Our capability with words outweighed the risks associated with anatomical quirkiness in *Homo sapiens*. This capability could not have evolved unless the dog, whose sensory capacity compensated for our own lack, evolved with us at the same time.

Competition

The fossils of our early ancestors show that our evolutionary predecessors were naturally selected to be in tune with their environment, for they changed explicably as the environment changed. Our early ancestors were powerful, probably had fine sensory powers, probably had rather easier births, probably were less likely to choke and probably did not have impacted wisdom teeth. Over a long period of time, as the various species evolved, their brain size gradually increased through a process called neoteny, which will be explained later. This meant their infants were dependent for some years. As a result, the core families needed to take refuge in caves. The availability of caves would have been a limiting resource for their survival. Then, as now, a really good cave was something to die for. For some two million years or more they depended on caves for protection against a plethora of predators, while mothers helped each other give birth and then raised infants over several years until they too could help defend the cave and find food for the group.

This book accepts the Neandertal[2] (*Homo*

2. The way "Neandertal" is spelt here may be a little confusing, since in many texts the "h" in "...thal.." is retained. The species was named after the Neander Valley. At that time a "valley" was called a "thal". Hence "*Homo neanderthalensis*". Then, with one of those flourishing strokes of the bureaucratic pen, a valley became spelt as "tal" on maps and Neanderthal lost its "h". This book follows the later convention of dropping the "h" in general discussion.

neanderthalensis) as the most likely penultimate *Homo* species. There were most likely two other *Homo* species in the background as we *Homo sapiens* evolved, *Homo floresiensis* (the little Indonesian hobbit) and a third whose skeleton is being classified. However, the Neandertal was our most serious competitor.

The last known Neandertal group became extinct about 28,500 years ago, holed up in caves in the far reaches of Western Europe. The species finally had been displaced by *Homo sapiens*. The Neandertal was an animal species one would expect to evolve, according to the conservative process of natural selection. It walked upright, made fire and used tools that it manufactured. It was organised, brawny, brainy and nosey. It was social and undoubtedly could communicate within the group by language. The head of the adult Neandertal was larger proportioned than ours. It held a more voluminous brain in a flatter cranium and had a much larger face and nose, and the "muzzle" part of its face jutted forward. Its head probably had not rotated as far as ours and was not domed, so Neandertal mothers would have an easier time at birth than our mothers do. Its muzzle suggests a good sense of smell and the Neandertal must have been alert and observant (Fee, fo, fie, fum, I smell the blood of a Wordy One!).

The Neandertal was not as good an organiser as we are. This shows it was not quite as bright as we are although its brain was as voluminous as ours, often even larger. Therefore, one can guess that some of the volume of its brain was attributable to large olfactory bulbs servicing its big nasal area. The jutting face and very large, chinless jaws were supported by hefty shoulder and neck muscles. Within its cavernous mouth its teeth were well spaced; it did not suffer from impacted wisdom teeth. Its tongue most likely lolled more freely than ours does and so the Neandertal probably lacked verbal precision.

There is much to respect about the Neandertal as a product of the conservative process of evolution by means of natural selection. Yet *Homo neanderthalensis* was surpassed by *Homo sapiens*, a puny human being with much reduced olfactory power. How could this be?

Co-evolution

The answer is that the forebears of *Homo sapiens* were forearmed because they were forewarned against the Neandertal. As the *Homo* species became brainier, it evolved better organisation and its caves became rich niches that the ancestors of several other animals began to exploit for food and shelter. Those animals included the ancestor of the dog, which began to adapt to life with *Homo*. At some point in time, the forebears of *Homo sapiens* became aware of the ancestral dog as a sentinel. These forebears were variants of a *Homo* population. They had slightly larger brains than the average and, consequently, because of rotation of the heavier head, slightly flatter faces and reduced sense of smell, but they had slightly better enunciation. Their olfactory deficiency was covered by their exploitation of the dogs' sense of smell. Those cave-people who were better communicators would tend to become more numerous, as would their genes.

The proposition being laid before you is that co-evolution of a complex had begun that would see relatively enormous olfactory bulbs of the brain located in the dog and relatively enormous cerebral hemispheres of the brain located in human beings, who consequently had better anatomy for speech (and more to talk about).

The discussion in the book centres mainly on the sense of smell, but human survival continues to depend upon other complementary sensory powers in the dog as well. An anecdote from the major war in Vietnam illustrates the point. Rod Reeve was a colleague of mine who has devoted his life to the delivery of aid for international development and for emergencies. This involved a lot of travel. A decade or so ago, when he learnt I was interested in the relationship between people and dogs, Rod told me this: During one of his many visits to Laos, he was told by a woman that, during the war, B52 bombers returning from missions in Vietnam unloaded any unused bombs over Laos, in the vicinity of the Ho Chi Minh trail. They could not return to base carrying bombs, as it would be too dangerous if they were to crash on landing. The bombers were at such high altitude that people living in the vicinity of the trail had no warning of the jettisoned bombs but, when they saw their dogs running for the caves into which they had moved for refuge from hostilities, they also ran for the caves. According to the Laotian woman, without the dogs as sentinels, their group could hardly have survived.

There are many such anecdotes, I know, but the reference to caves resonates with co-evolution of cave people and cave dogs.

The Composite Conversationalist

Many ideas have been absorbed to develop the argument above: When animals evolve as a complex, the whole may be a greater evolutionary success than its parts alone. This book is about the evolution of the complex of people and dogs. A corollary of Charles Darwin's explanation of natural selection is that interaction between species can affect their evolution, but natural selection cannot modify a species, without giving it any advantage, for the good of another species. The Composite Conversationalist has existed since humans and dogs came into being, and it still exists wherever people and dogs are today. It is ubiquitous in time and place. The Composite Conversationalist can be found in the caves of the Cro-Magnon, with the Sumerians, the Egyptians, in Biblical references and Chinese temples. It is both a defender of territory and a coloniser of new territory. It is an explorer and can be found in tropical jungles, deserts and Arctic wastes; it values refuge and prospect and can be found in villages, transhumances, suburbs and swanky city apartments. The Composite Conversationalist is an example of the Darwinian "melting together" of two species.

Since the discovery of the gene as the unit of inheritance a new discourse on natural selection became necessary: Neo-Darwinism. Richard Dawkins is a British writer who has done much to explain and popularise Neo-Darwinism. In a series of books he viewed natural selection occurring at the level of genes, both selfish and selfless, the genes competing with other genes for places in chromosomes in the nucleus of the cells of plants and animals. A gene is an extraordinary molecule that can determine the characteristics of an organism. A gene in one organism can also influence the characteristics of another organism, so long as the survival of both is enhanced. This is a Neo-Darwinian interpretation of Darwin's corollary mentioned in the paragraph above. Richard Dawkins developed this idea into his *The Extended Phenotype: the gene as the unit of selection*, which he published in 1982.

A "phenotype" is defined in *The Penguin Dictionary of Biology* as "the sum of the characteristics manifested by an organism". The genotype of an organism, on the other hand, is the total of genes in each of the cells of an organism. The expression of the genotype may be influenced by the environment of the organism; hence the phenotype may not be a complete reflection of the genotype. This book argues that the Composite Conversationalist is an extended phenotype.

The publications of Philip Lieberman and Steven Pinker helped me to understand the anatomy of our head compared with that of the dog, in relation to speech, and then propose that people and dogs evolved as an extended phenotype.

Exaptation is an idea that also is at the heart of the Composite Conversationalist Hypothesis. You are unlikely to find "exaptation" in a dictionary; it is a word invented by Stephen Jay Gould and Elizabeth Vrba to better convey the concept that an adaptation evolved in one environment might prime organisms to adapt in another. Already mentioned above is an example of speech exaptation, that is, the likely connection between our heavy, brainy head necessarily rotating to balance better on a more upright spinal column and the way the face then dropped and became smaller, leading to a smaller bite and facilitating enunciation. I found the writings of Lloyd DuBrul, Leslie Aiello and Jeffrey Laitman most helpful in understanding this exaptation.

The psychologist Robin Dunbar proposed that grooming exapted primates to evolve language as an efficient form of social grooming as groups increased in size, particularly within the groups which had grooming/gossiping females at the core. Peter MacNeilage, also a psychologist, argued how the operational limitations of vocal folds would become an exaptation for forming syllables in human speech, and how evolution of the brain to permit advancing communication in primates and others could become an exaptation of the human brain to conceive and perceive form and content in words and hence lead to speech.

The authors mentioned here do not include those whose painstaking descriptions of field data and brilliant reviews of the literature were also read. They are too numerous to mention at this stage. Collectively, all those thinkers showed that the power of natural selection is wonderful, but not mysterious.

Research proceeds on the genes of species, within the general concept of evolution by natural selection. Genes are linked in thread-like chromosomes, each species having a particular number of chromosomes in the nucleus of each of their cells. The package of chromosomes in the nucleus is the genome of that species. A review by Graham Lawton for *New Scientist* in 2009 described how certain organisms that have multiple life stages may be fusions of different genomes, each operating a stage in the lifecycle of, for example, insects that have larvae, pupae and sexually mature forms.

In the light of the *New Scientist's* astonishing proposition, it seems quite modest to propose that the dog, with its marvellous sense of smell, was an integral part of the evolution of *Homo sapiens*' capacity for speech, because some variants of *Homo* with dropped faces became aware of the usefulness of the dog as a sentinel and survived to out-compete the Neandertal. It seems quite modest to propose that the capacity of *Homo sapiens* to organise because of improving speech provided an increasingly productive niche in which the dog could multiply. It seems quite modest to conclude that it is part of human nature to associate with dogs and part of dog nature to associate with people.

The following chapters deal with the evolution of the Composite Conversationalist, beginning with a brief discussion of the theory of natural selection, then mention of the geological epoch that powered evolutionary change in the ancestors of the Composite Conversationalist. Then following is discussion on how *Homo* species evolved along a rationally explicable trajectory. There is comment on the radical differentiation of *Homo sapiens* with particular reference to speech and sense of smell. There is comment on how our evolution ran away with us, as Christopher Wills put it in relation to the brain, which he saw operating in a feed back loop whereby increased intelligence leads to increased complexity, leads to increased intelligence, and so on, and so on .... Chapters then deal with the speciation of the dog in the *Homo* cave; of complementarities it shares with its co-evolutionary partner; and of its natural place in today's world. In the final chapter I conclude that the Composite Conversationalist is a natural phenomenon.

Chapter Two - Basic Theory

Players in Life's chancy game,
Never remain quite the same;
Those marshalling Reason's tools,
They might figure out the rules.

When one opens a newspaper or a journal, or turns on the television news, it is likely that yet another amazing breakthrough in the study of genetics is being reported. Entire genotypes of species are being listed and studied, beginning with the human genome. Genes carry information coded in molecules of deoxyribonucleic acid (DNA), and are the means by which specific characteristics are passed on to succeeding generations. The genes of the human genome have been described in a years-long internationally collaborative project.

Attempts also are being made to describe the genome of the Neandertal using analysis of DNA found in remnants of tissue. Neandertal DNA has been found in the human genome, suggesting hybridisation of the two species. In scientific journals, papers describing sequences of genes are now written by teams of a dozen or more collaborators and are as long as books. Claims and counter-claims are made as to when species differentiated from ancestral stock. Sensational headlines suggest that each new discovery shakes the Darwinian tree, even uprooting it, because some flawed statement has been exposed in one of Charles Darwin's many books, or in his personal notebooks.

Natural Selection

Charles Darwin argued in a massive essay, published in 1859, that species originate by means of natural selection in a continuous, gradual process. Of course, even the fittest individual can be unlucky, the unfit can be lucky, mutations occur, founders greedily guard harems and beget frantically, genetic drift is mathematically inevitable, sexual selection can yield bizarre results and quantum mechanics might carry our genes off into a parallel universe. There are arguments about what is gradual or not, and about continuity.

But, as Richard Dawkins noted, Darwin's theory remains the only theory that explains organised complexity in living organisms. It is Charles Darwin's theory which has been adopted as the overarching principle for discussion in this book.

Charles Darwin's life work was immense. His argument for natural selection in the *Origin of Species* is almost 700 pages long. A statement from that argument is copied below.

"Can it, then, be thought improbable, seeing that variations useful to man have undoubtedly occurred, that other variations useful in some way to each being in the great and complex battle for life, should occur in the course of many successive generations? If such do occur, can we doubt (remembering that many more individuals are born than can survive) that individuals having any advantage, however slight, over others, would have the best chance of surviving and of procreating their kind? On the other hand, we may feel sure that any variation in the least degree injurious would be rigidly destroyed. This preservation of favourable individual differences and variations, and the destruction of those which are injurious, I have called Natural Selection, or the Survival of the Fittest. Variations neither useful nor injurious would not be affected by natural selection, and would be left either a fluctuating element, as perhaps we see in certain polymorphic species, or would ultimately become fixed, owing to the nature of the organism and the nature of the conditions." (page 98, sixth edition, 1901)

This marvellous passage of prose is among the most important ever written. A minimalist summary by Ford Doolittle is that natural selection is the differential reproduction of variants, and Paul Leyhausen points out that "survival of the fitting" is also a productive way of understanding the process of natural selection. For Charles Darwin, the struggle for existence occurred because populations increase such that more individuals are born than can survive, and hence there must be a struggle to survive within species, or between species or because of environmental constraints. The contestants are not aware of any "struggle"; this is an explanatory term to illustrate the inexorable changing of the guard over generations of time that occurs in nature.

On matters of detail the simple proposition of natural selection soon becomes complicated. For example, some characteristics may be more heritable than others, and naturally selective pressures may vary in intensity such that, in a wildly fluctuating environment, species become extinct or new ones originate rapidly or, alternatively, in long periods of calm little change in species occurs.

The idea in this book is speculative and so it seems impractical to delve deeply into detail. The basic concept of natural selection is sufficient to move the argument along, with some qualifications dealt with below. However, it may be noted at this time that the environment of an animal also will change as other animals and plants in that environment evolve and change. The complexity of the organic dynamism of the relationships requires a philosophical appreciation as much as a structure of particulate facts, especially as the relationships may be evolved dependencies.

Darwin was conscious of heritable interdependencies in nature, for he wrote on how the English humble-bee, red clover and heartsease plants were interdependent. In such cases, however, he pointed out that natural selection could not modify one species for the good of another species unless the survival of both species was enhanced. It is therefore interesting that, according to Loren Eiseley who wrote a biography of Darwin, when the Duke of Argyll (in *Primeval Man* 1869) argued that natural selection could not have applied to human beings since we are clearly quite puny and unfit for survival, Darwin did not think of co-evolution with another species, but wriggled out of the argument by suggesting our evolution may have occurred in some out of the way haven where our puniness was in some way beneficial. Darwin could have mentioned, in the same way that this book mentions people and dogs, that a complex of animals whose parts were "cooperating" might become an organism or phenotype which would be fit for survival.

Charles Darwin was not aware of genes. Their discovery lay a hundred years in the future. Neo-Darwinism recognises the gene as the unit of evolution and updates the discourse based on Darwin's concepts. As already mentioned, one of the most effective writers within this discourse is Richard Dawkins, who wrote a number of important books that made Neo-Darwinism accessible to a broad readership. Examples are *The Blind Watchmaker* and *The Selfish Gene*. For him, as genes compete with like genes for a place on the chromosomes of a species, the animal thus becomes "a survival machine built by a short-lived confederation of long-lived genes".

The Extended Phenotype

It may be remembered that a phenotype is the sum of the characteristics manifested by an organism and that it was Richard Dawkins who coined the term "extended phenotype" in his book of the same name. He argued that the genes in one organism effect heritable changes in the behaviour and morphology of another organism. His statement, "an animal's behaviour tends to maximise the survival of the genes 'for' that behaviour, whether or not those genes happen to be in the body of the particular animal performing it", was an enormous insight into the complexity and interconnectedness of natural processes. In the *Ancestor's Tale*, which he wrote with Yan Wong, he described the way genes in the beaver that cause its dam-building behaviour also create the phenotype that is the particular dam. The dam is an ecosystem within which other species adapt and therefore it affects their evolution.

This book argues that people and dogs are extended phenotypes, but not in quite the way Richard Dawkins has suggested. Rather, the research of Calaway Dodson is offered as a better contextual example. A specific orchid puts out a scent that attracts the males of one species of bee, who collect the components of the fragrance in cavities in their hind legs. The fragrance attracts other males of the species and they form a single specific group, which in turn attracts the female and mating takes place. The fragrance is thus a way of identifying and concentrating a single bee species among many bees, and the reproduction of that species is enhanced naturally. Similarly, the attraction of the fragrance for this species of bee means that the pollen adhering to the bees is carried to orchids of the same species as the pollen giver. The situation is complex and organised by natural selection. The specific bee and the orchid are extended phenotypes. Their relationship is mutually beneficial, and so is symbiotic, but it is a special form of symbiosis because the bee and the orchid have become interdependent and co-evolutionary.

It may be seen from the example above that the interdependency is beneficial until there is some environmental change that endangers one, and thus the other, partner in the unit.

Exaptation

Another useful explanatory term is "exaptation[1]" invented by Elizabeth Vrba and Stephen Jay Gould in 1982 to better convey the concept that an adaptation evolved in one environment might fortuitously prepare a population of organisms to adapt in another. It is not a pre-adaptation, for it is impossible for an organism to foresee a need that might arise in the course of natural selection. Elizabeth Vrba used the example of horns, which evolved for defence, becoming equally

1. Loren Eiseley tells us that Alfred Russel Wallace had grasped the idea of exaptation when he noted that "savages" had developed the capacity for speech in anticipation of becoming learned. By this time, 10 years after publication of *Origin*, Wallace had begun to doubt that the human brain had been naturally selected, to Darwin's dismay.

important for survival because they identified and attracted mates. Feathers that evolved for insulation might prepare an animal for flight. Stephen Gould saw evolution occurring in fits and starts (punctuated equilibriums) when adaptations became exaptations that took the animal to a next tier in development. While it is arguable that punctuation actually occurs, exaptation is a powerful metaphor that has been adopted in this book to help describe the anatomical and behavioural changes that occurred in people and dogs as they co-evolved.

"Domestication"

In this book I argue that people and dogs are animals who co-evolved, therefore it is not appropriate to describe the dog as created by or for people and call it domesticated, except in a loose and unimaginative way. A naturalistic perspective shows the dog to be a species originating in a natural habitat that was the *Homo* cave. Its natural habitat remains human organisation. Certainly, "domesticatability" is a trait that characterised the ancestral dog and one which would be naturally selected and developed as the dog co-evolved with evolving people. The result is a species in its own right, and it is misleading to regard the dog as a subspecies of wolf (with the inference that it could somehow regress if wolves ever got off the endangered lists and began mating with dogs energetically), just as it would be misleading to regard the various wolves as subspecies of dog that could be domesticated. The more liberal comment that the dog somehow "domesticated us" is also misleading: Nobody *did* anything to anybody. Two animals co-evolved naturally in a shared ecological niche and, over time, became *Homo sapiens* and *Canis familiaris*.

Later chapters will discuss more fully taking the "dog" out of the dogma about domestication. Now, however, we can move on to Chapter Three and briefly outline the factors that drove the evolution of our ancestors and our own evolution. Emphasis is placed upon the climatic changes in the past three million years or so, but it will be realised that the importance of these changes is not only the direct effect they had on our ancestors' survival, but also the way the changes affected the plants and prey/predator animal species in our ancestors' environments. The changes were more extreme than at present and naturally selective pressures for the origination and extinction of species were therefore also more extreme. The climatic effects on the evolution of fauna and flora were particularly marked in the higher northern latitudes. The effects were less in the warmer, lower northern latitudes and south of the equator.

Chapter Three - Climate Change

Lifestyle choices were exchanged,
As the icy climates changed;
The Adaptive Imperative,
Selected those that could not live.

In Chapter Two, Charles Darwin asked us to remember that one of the conditions for natural selection is that many more individuals are born than can survive. Such excessive procreation can be absolute, as when hundreds of juveniles are hatched, of which few survive. Excess can also be relative to resources even when only a few young are born. In our ancestors' case, for example, it is hard to imagine the species existing in very large numbers, given that they had newly adopted a terrestrial existence. But the critical resources they required may have been relatively scarce.

For simplicity, our ancestors will be referred to as *Homo* or *Homo* species where possible, to avoid the esoteric differentiation of "hominids", "hominins" and *Homo* species that can be confusing, particularly when consulting different age brackets of literature.

For *Homo* species, caves must have been a critical resource for shelter, because of the strategy of neoteny upon which the species was embarked. They would have been contested by other *Homo* species and cave-dwelling species such as the cave bear and other predators. Caves would thus have been relatively scarce. The problem of scarcity of caves would be compounded by ever longer periods of infant dependency requiring the resource to be available and contested perhaps for generations. Large predators must have exerted pressure on *Homo* populations and accentuated the need for caves.

Food and water were of course essential resources. Fluctuations in their availability would force *Homo* populations to adapt accordingly or perish. Loren Eiseley tells us that when Darwin returned from his voyage around the world as the naturalist aboard HMS *Beagle* under the command of Captain Fitz Roy, he had realised that the varying offspring of all species in a particular spot would tend to fill all ecological niches. Whether *Homo* were numerous or not, they too would be caught up in this competition for the resources for survival. This tendency to exploit resources became known as the Law of Divergence, which dictated the adaptive radiation of species. As for all other species, *Homo* evolution was dynamic, fraught, difficult and not at all idyllic.

The overall influence on this dynamic was climate change. It is therefore necessary to look briefly at the climatic factors that influenced the evolution of *Homo* species. The species that will be discussed include the Australopithecine, or the Southern Apes, who strictly speaking are not *Homo* species. In the next section, grudging reference will therefore be made to "hominids" to include the Australopithecine.

Winds of Change

The human component of the Composite Conversationalist of today is the product of enormous changes, climatic and tectonic, over millions of years. Although some of the early evolution of the hominids occurred in the Pliocene subdivision of the Tertiary Period, the vast bulk of their evolution occurred in the latest Quaternary (Fourth) Period of geological time, and most of the hominid story unfolds over the Pleistocene Epoch of that Period.

Richard F. Flint in *Britannica* provides a useful summary of change in that epoch. His summary introduces the idea that climate change most likely was an important factor in the evolution of *Homo* species.

The Pleistocene spanned from about three million years to 10,000 years ago. Hominid evolution continues from the Pleistocene through the next epoch, the Holocene, through to the present. Hominids waddled more-or-less upright into the Pleistocene as Southern Apes (Australopithecine) and strode out of it as Wise Men (*Homo sapiens*), leaving behind them the remains of the several hominid species who had not survived the journey.

The Pleistocene may also be known as the Ice Ages or the Glacial Age. Vast sheets of ice and glaciers were not unique to this epoch, but the Pleistocene was characterized by the extent to which the immense sheets of ice, up to three kilometres thick, spread south into the middle latitudes of the northern hemisphere, reaching present-day locations of London, Amsterdam, New York, and down to northern Italy and southern Russia. Smaller glaciers ground away further south, in the mountains of southern Europe, Africa, Japan and even at the Equator. The presence of glaciers so far south was rare in other geological periods. In response to fluctuations in the Earth's climate, ice sheets and glaciers melted and rebuilt, causing a series of cooler glacial and warmer interglacial cycles within the epoch. As the ice spread or contracted, ocean levels changed, "temporary" lakes were formed and then dried out, and the fauna and flora changed in nature and extent. The climate generally was cooler than the present, with summer average temperatures perhaps five to seven degrees Celsius less than now. Snow persisted at lower altitudes than it does today.

The ice sheets and glaciers were so massive that their weight distorted and depressed the Earth's crust, which rose again during interglacial periods. The weight even caused bulging of the crust at the margins of the ice sheets. Since glaciers then held much more water than now, sea levels may have been 100 metres lower than at present. Evaporation of sea water fed the glaciers and was returned to the seas in warmer periods as river run-off. However, since much of the water remained held as ice, the refreshed sea levels may have been only 20 to 40 metres higher, still lower than today. Thus at periods in the Pleistocene, present-day islands, such as the British Isles, the western Indonesian Archipelago and those in Bering Strait remained connected to continents such that animals (including hominids) could move to and fro. A broad coastal plain existed from southern Africa around the Indian Ocean to Indonesia. Australia and New Guinea were connected. The cycles also affected levels of water in rivers and lakes, and affected wind patterns.

The Pleistocene was a dynamic epoch for species of animals and plants, the ranges of which changed as climate changed. Cooler periods saw animal species drift south towards the equator and from higher to lower altitudes. These effects were less in regions not affected directly by ice sheets, such as East Africa where much of the hominid story was enacted. The accumulation of effects also affected the deposition and location of fossils and the (un)likelihood that they would be found by present-day paleontologists (fossil hunters).

Climatic fluctuations thus exerted strong evolutionary pressures on animals in the Pleistocene and resulted in the origin of new species or the migration of species. For example, only six of 119 mammal species that now exist in Eurasia existed in the earlier Pliocene. Other changes to the animals' environment included movements of the Earth's crust, which built massive mountain ranges, such as the Himalayas. These lifted up ecosystems into colder altitudes. They acted as partitions and barriers to the movement of animals, perhaps causing them to adapt and form new species, and also changed patterns of the climate itself. In the Pleistocene, periods of high rainfall turned the Sahara and Kalahari, and other deserts in Brazil, India and Australia, into moist savannas. At other times arid conditions applied and major rivers such as the Nile dwindled and dried.

Therefore glacial and interglacial cycles were powerhouses of evolutionary change in the Pleistocene. Species adapted or radiated to become new species. If they did not adapt, they became extinct. Paleontologists have most actively studied European faunas. There, they have found, new groups of animals evolved such that the mid-Pleistocene can be said to have had its own distinctive fauna. Of course, we and our ancestors and relatives were part of the Pleistocene fauna, as was the other protagonist in this story, the dog, along with its ancestors and relatives. During the Pleistocene, we and our relatives adapted through behavioural and cultural changes, such as wearing skins, controlling fire, seeking refuge in caves and organising to handle the threats and opportunities that these behaviours implied to our survival. As will be explained, the adaptations were enhanced and constrained by our biology and the process of natural selection.

The variety of flora and fauna in Pleistocene Europe was amazing. Eighty per cent of the plants presently in north-western Europe existed in the Pleistocene. Rhinoceroses, mammoths, elephants and musk oxen insulated with woolly coats, polar bears insulated with blubber, reindeer, moose, lemmings and, in the early part of the epoch, straight-tusked elephants and hippopotamuses abounded. In the Americas, zebra-like horses and camel forms appeared, as did mammoths, other horses, musk oxen, antelopes and rodents, bison, skunks and bats. Not specifically mentioned in the list are birds and waterfowl, presumably because they left no traces in the fossil record, and also marine animals, but these must have been important food sources for the hominids, if modern human hunter-gatherers are a guide to the past.

The Pleistocene was also characterised by a high level of extinction of species, since up to 70 per cent of mammals went extinct in northern America. Fewer became extinct in Eurasia, Africa and southern America. Extinctions of marsupial species in Australia were marked. The Australian conservationist and scientist Tim Flannery attributes this to the arrival in Australia of *Homo sapiens*, who "ate the future" of many marsupial species by killing them or out-competing them. His argument was that there had been no opportunity for a natural balance to develop between people and the Australian marsupials, unlike in the African situation, for example, where people and prey/predator animals had evolved together. I think the dog arrived with the earliest *Homo sapiens* and played its part in eating the future of the marsupials.

In continents other than Australia, naturally changing environments may have caused the extinctions of animals, but *Homo sapiens* has also been blamed for mass killing of many animal species directly and by adversely affecting the environment in which they lived, for example, through clearing forests and so causing erosion and land degradation. Archeologist David Miles has suggested that in the late Pleistocene at Star Carr in Yorkshire, United Kingdom, clearing of forests by people was a way of encouraging grazing by target prey species and was a prelude to a move to agriculture. Tim Flannery points to the deliberate stocking of islands in Melanesia with the cuscus (a tree dwelling marsupial similar in appearance to a possum) by people as early as 20,000 years ago. In other words, the seeds of agriculture were sown by the rational behaviour of hunter-gathers rather than broadcast in a later revolution of technology from the Levant.

As mitigation for the charge that people caused mass extinctions of animals, it has also been argued that there simply were not enough early people to do the damage for which they have been blamed. An argument that counters that positivist view is that some animals (camels, for example) should have been well adapted for climate change, yet became extinct.

Many authorities argue that we are still in the Pleistocene, that is, it continues into the present. But the present has been named the Holocene to recognise the advent of human kind and its evident impact on the environment. This Epoch began 10,000 years ago. Perhaps the Holocene was given its own name as a polite acknowledgement of the Western theist discourse that was the orthodoxy of the 1800s.

The Holocene Epoch thus can be seen as constructed by god-respecting scientists to allow the appraisal of God's work to date and what it meant to be human. Certainly there is no reason to think that the Glacial Age is over: We currently are in the latest interglacial interval of the Quaternary Period. Human beings were likely having an impact on their environment well before 10,000 years ago, as discussed above, but in the Holocene human beings may have been responsible for the extinction of legendary animals such as the cave bear, woolly mammoth and great elk. It may also be that these animals had so specialised for cold-climate environments that they could not adapt to the current warmer interglacial interval. The question is moot: Sea at the present levels has flooded much of what otherwise might have been found by paleontologists and archeologists.

The brief outline given above shows that our genes have been selected in a natural environment that was quite extreme compared to the present. This was especially the case in the higher latitudes, but must still have been marked even in equatorial Africa, at certain times. In succeeding chapters the emphasis is on the evolution of anatomical changes that led to us becoming loquacious dog-keepers, but it should be borne in mind that the natural environment alternated between sweltering heat and freezing cold, between want and plenty. The alternations forced evolutionary change in us *Homo*, our food and our predators.

Chapter Four - Caves

Species with the best finesse
Had brains and nosiness;
For years-a-million-plus,
Centre stage was erectus.

There is much debate on the relationship that various ancestors in the hominid lineage had with modern human beings. There is uncertainty about names and categories, and times of occurrence of various species. Indeed, there is a fairly rich history of active disagreement among paleontologists on both central principles and details. This is not unexpected because the intense public interest in our origins encourages speculation about the small body of evidence that has been obtained, often with difficulty and under dangerous conditions. This book joins in that speculation unabashedly.

Although the picture is being enhanced by the analysis of genes at the molecular level, it is not necessarily clarified, because there often is disagreement on the interpretation of results. As far as is practicable I shall not enter this debate, but take, on face value, those results that appear to fit within the logic of natural selection. My aim is to simplify the argument, not complicate it with dialectics. To do so I have chosen four species to act as waypoints indicative of human evolution in the discussion in the next few chapters: *Australopithecus afarensis*, *Homo erectus*, *Homo heidelbergensis* and *Homo neanderthalensis.* For those who like the cut and thrust of debate, James Shreeve's *The Neandertal Enigma: solving the mystery of human origins* is an interesting beginning.

The following table has been sourced from Richard Leakey's *The Origin of Humankind*, as a guide to timelines in human evolution.

10 to 5 million years ago	Origin of bipedalism in Africa
4 to 3 million years ago	Earliest known fossils of human ancestors
3 to 2 million years ago	Origin of brain expansion, earliest known stone tools (found in Africa)
2 to 1 million years ago	*Homo erectus* expands out of Africa into Asia, major advance in tool manufacture (the Aechulean age), evidence of meat eating
1 million to 100,000 years ago	First use of fire, major advance in tool manufacture (the Mousterian age), origin of modern human beings
100,000 to 10,000 years ago	First evidence of art, agricultural revolution
10,000 years ago to the present	First cities, industrial revolution, technological revolution

Ardipithecus ramidus are presently thought to be the earliest probable human ancestors. They were named to indicate the likely branching of African apes and proto-human beings. *Ardipithecus ramidus* occurred about 4.5 million years ago. We need not dally with them. We need only to thank *Ardipithecus* for being there for us, and move on.

Juicy Lucy and Others

At the Australian Museum in Sydney a diorama was set up of a leopard dragging the body of an Australopithecine (Southern Ape) into a tree by its head. The fangs of the leopard had penetrated the skull and the body dangled lifelessly from its jaws. The leopard was expressionless and looked introspective in the way cats do when they first catch an animal. To me, the Australopithecine seemed abject and tragic. I identified with it, and felt for it. It was simply prey. Yet it was the forerunner of a species that would come to call itself dominant.

That Australopithecine was our relative to the nth degree. Australopithecine were small and relatively defenseless hominids who showed human-like qualities such as bipedalism and increased brain size for their body weight. Australopithecine brains were about the same size as that of a modern chimpanzee, but their average encephalisation quotient (the relationship between brain weight, body weight and a constant factor), as calculated by Alan Walker and Pat Shipman in *The Wisdom of Bones,* was a little higher, at about 3.0. The average encephalisation quotient for a modern human being is around 7.3.

What we know of Australopithecine is based on fossil evidence. Only one collection of Australopithecine fossils is complete enough to be called a skeleton, and that belongs to an *Australopithecus afarensis* discovered in Ethiopia in 1974, called Lucy by her discoverers. Lucy lived about three million years ago. Although she was human-like, her fossil rib cage had the conical, pot-bellied shape of the apes, indicating it was unlikely she could control her breathing sufficiently to make very complex vocalisation. She was small. Forty-seven of her fossilised bones were found. They indicated she was about 1.2 metres short. Other skeletons suggested that the average size of *A. afarensis* was 1.5 metres height and 65 kilograms weight for the males and one metre and 30 kilograms for the females.

Yves Coppens is a paleontologist who suggested in *East of Eden* that the vast tectonic movements that formed the Rift Valley in Africa physically split the climate of the area into wetter and drier regions. The ancestors of the hominids were also split, those in wetter regions evolving into African apes, while those in drier regions to the east evolved into hominids (eventually to become human). Remnants of ulna and humerus (arm bones) and other fossils indicated that these hominids climbed trees, and also walked on two legs. From the period of around 3.5 million years ago, the evolution of these hominids appeared to have remained stable, and bipedalism was not accompanied by significant brain expansion for as long as 1.7 million years. The Australopithecine had adapted successfully to life in the savannas. Here their diets included harder nuts and fruits than those in the forests. Powerful chewing teeth evolved as an adaptation to this diet. Bipedalism freed their hands better for more efficient gathering of food such as seeds and leaves, and also helped the Australopithecine to develop skills with simple weapons. Hand-held weapons reduced selection pressure for large canine teeth and smaller canine teeth were an exaptation for efficient side-to-side chewing.

The hominids' tree-living, arboreal capacities allowed them to gather food from the trees. Of probable additional importance is the likelihood that the trees provided safer sleeping places and refuges from the large, swift, social carnivores that preyed upon them. The hominids were under a great deal of predation pressure. Among the predators were two hyena and three sabre-toothed cat species that would have easily outmatched the Australopithecine. It is quite likely that leopards also preyed on hominids. Packs of social canids such as *Lycaon* the wild dog may also have preyed upon them and influenced the evolution of Australopithecine. Indeed, the presence of large predators must have influenced the way all our later ancestors evolved.

Brain development is not possible without an increase in the size of the cranium. While the hominids' lifestyles remained anchored by refuges in trees, a very large cranium could not develop, because the necessarily heavy head would interfere with balance and agility. Large-headed infants would require a long period of dependency, which would endanger their mothers in the trees. Marked postnatal brain growth in arboreal progeny most likely could not occur because it would imply a long and highly immature neonatal state, with the offspring clinging to the mother and so reducing her chance of survival.

On the other hand, bipedalism also had advantages over arboreal agility when it came to survival. Pat Shipman is a paleontologist who investigated whether vegetarian hominids might also have developed a taste for meat as they became more terrestrial. She argued that bipedalism was efficient for walking; for increasing the hominids' fields of view for safety and for finding food; and for carrying things. Using scanning electron microscopy, Pat Shipman painstakingly compared cut marks on fossil bones of prey animals utilised by hominids and carnivore predators, with marks on bones of animals killed by Neolithic hunters in Kenya 2300 years ago. She found that hominids most likely were actually scavenging whatever they could – meat, skin or tendon – rather than killing the large animals and dismembering them. From that perspective, she concluded that since bipedalism was better for sustained walking to search an area, rather than for short bursts of fast running to catch prey, it was an adaptation for scavenging, as was the upright posture an adaptation that aided searching. The things that were carried, she thought, most likely were simple stone tools for smashing, scraping and cutting, rather than parts of carcass. After all, a hominid carrying meat would be harassed by predators. Interestingly, Pat Shipman noted that fearsome specialist predators, such as the sabre-toothed cats and ancient cheetahs, were ill adapted for crunching bones. Because the cats could eat only the large, soft, juicy bits of their prey, they would have been generous donors of leftovers for our scavenging forebears. As will be shown below, adapting to meat eating by the vegetarian hominids was an exaptation for brain growth, since the brain requires a diet high in protein. Becoming an omnivore was thus an exaptation for the survival of brainy descendants who would, as we shall see, migrate globally through different and changing environments.

At this point I ask that you pause for thought. Most primates do not have a notable sense of smell; the human being is a particular sluggard in this regard. But a vegetarian hominid on the way to being a meat-eating scavenger on the savanna had better start evolving olfactory prowess to detect carrion and for self-protection. From its bipedal vantage point that same primate would also begin evolving an awareness of the wider picture, noting the activity of vultures to indicate the position of a carcass, for example. Naturally, variants with a nose for things and a bit of nous would be selected for survival. Unsurprisingly, the fossil record arguably shows that our ancestors (but not ourselves) were progressively more notable for their nosiness as well as braininess.

Charles Kimberlin Brain was a model practitioner of the art of studying assemblages of buried fossils, called taphonomy. His *The Hunters or the Hunted? An introduction to African cave taphonomy* remains a guide to the careful, intelligent unearthing of fossils by digging through layers of cave detritus according to a grid system. Brain also studied and compared the feeding habits of various living predators, to gain an appreciation of the way in which bones may be left after a kill. He realised that survival of bones as fossil relics was due largely to both the characteristics of the bones themselves and to the feeding habits of the predators. For example, light bones and cartilage would not survive and also, if it was the nature of predators to eat particular bones such as vertebrae, these would not appear in the fossil record. During a 30-year-long project in the Swartskrans cave in the Sterkfontein valley in South Africa, Brain found that the newly terrestrial Australopithecine had been preyed upon by specialised predators that had adapted for that purpose.

With this grisly information in mind, it is not difficult to imagine the horrors of the African nights for the hominids. The zebra, for instance, is a much larger animal than the Australopithecine. The zebra is a formidable animal. It is powerful; it can bite ferociously and kick accurately with great force, no doubt in part due to the evolutionary pressures exerted on it by predators. But at night, it cannot see to defend itself against lions or hyenas. Every night is fraught with deadly danger. For a zebra, having the ability to imagine the approaching night would be so stressful as to compromise its own survival. A vivid imagination in a zebra would be counter-survival.

Our early ancestors, on the other hand, were on the cusp of surviving by thinking their way into a future that included us as descendants. African nights for them must thus have been desperate indeed. The approach of every night must have been terrifying for them, as they crouched in the deepening dark. They were accessible by carnivores even if they took refuge in caves. How desperate must have been the race to organise protective strategies, or perish! We might pity our small, dimly self-aware ancestors – and yet, we are the living proof that they managed to survive.

Charles Kimberlin Brain discovered, in the cave he investigated so thoroughly, "the evolving men mastered a threat to their security that had been posed by the cave cats over countless generations ... the cats apparently controlled the Sterkfontein cave, dragging their Australopithecine victims into its dark recesses. (In time) however, the new men not only had evicted the predators, but had taken up residence in the very chamber where their ancestors had been eaten. How the people managed this is not recorded, but it could surely have been achieved only through increasing intelligence reflected in developing technology". At the very least, that technology might have been rational thought, perhaps resulting in a device as simple as a log dragged across the mouth of a cave at night, which then could be defended better with rudimentary weapons.

Control of fire and the use of stone weapons and tools would follow with the evolution of *Homo* species. Australopithecine of various species and *Homo* species coexisted for some time. According to Elizabeth Vrba, *Homo* species were generalist omnivores who could cope better with change. As mentioned above, there is considerable debate on the classification of the various *Homo* species. Some were very robust, others gracile. We can note that the variability that we inherited is the stuff upon which natural selection operates. Although Australopithecine are described above as using "tools", *Homo habilis* (Handyman) is generally considered to be the first of our ancestors to actually make stone tools. *Homo erectus* replaced *Homo habilis* about two million years ago. Both had larger brains and higher encephalisation quotients than the Australopithecine.

Homo erectus is our next waypoint, but before we meet them it is timely to discuss an important concept in human survival – neoteny.

Neoteny

As mentioned several times, increasing brain size is a feature of our successive ancestors. The need for a large head to accommodate an increasing brain has great evolutionary significance. Among other things, there is a limit, in a terrestrial animal, to how much the mother's pelvic channel can widen to pass a large-headed newborn without interfering with the locomotion and hence survival of the mother. Waddling away from pursuit by a predator simply will not do on the African savanna. The solution that evolved was the birthing of the infant well before it reached self-sufficient development. Stephen Jay Gould argued that neoteny (retarded somatic development) was a fundamental event in human evolution.

Clive Gamble in *Timewalkers* commented that a baby's brain at birth was only 25 per cent of the weight of an adult's, whereas that of a newborn chimpanzee was 46 per cent and that of a newborn macaque was 60 per cent of their adult brain weight. The remarkable extent to which crania and brains in human infants continued to develop after birth suggested that the same process occurred in our ancestors. Alan Walker and Pat Shipman in *The Wisdom of Bones* made the point that the modern human gestation period really is 21 months, not nine, because the brain of an infant continued to develop so markedly for a year after birth. Clive Gamble was even more emphatic: Although human, chimpanzee and macaque fetal brains grew at the same rate, the brain of a human infant continued to grow at the rapid fetal rate for two years and then at a slower rate for the next three years.

The size of an infant's head at birth (relative to the size of its mother's pelvic opening) and the length of time it was subsequently dependent on its mother, had important implications for the ways in which the species in our family could evolve.

Lengthy dependency of the young dictated that the adults developed formal social systems based on sharing. This was an adaptation that could be seen as an exaptation for evolving an instinct to explore, migrate and finally to colonise habitats. Reference will be made later to how the intense sociality of *Homo* life was an exaptation for spoken language, as group sizes increased.

I ask that you pause for thought again: When our ancestors were evicted from trees, they must have sheltered in caves or, at least, in burrows until they could find their dream cave. Families couldn't just huddle in groups through the long savanna nights. In the open, anything they could do, their predators could do much, much better. Until late in our history, when we could dominate our environment through fire and building substantial shelters and so on, our ancestors needed caves in which to rear their very demanding young. How would you handle a Terrible Two-year-old on the savanna? Ask a hyena to babysit? For much of human evolution, the home base must have been a cave. Cooperation in child rearing and in simply getting along together within the group in the cave must have been an imperative for survival, and so a naturally selected trait.

With this thought in mind, let us consider the next waypoint species, *Homo erectus.*

Nariokotome Boy – Bursting Out of His Genes

Nariokotome Boy was found on a hot, dusty day in August 1984, at Lake Turkana in northern Kenya. The National Geographic Society sponsored a dig in the dry bed of the Nariokotome River that runs into the lake. The leader of the team was Richard Leakey, a famous member of a famous family of paleoanthropologists. Other members of the team were a geologist, a paleontologist, and a number of keen-eyed Kenyan fossil spotters. Alan Walker was the paleontologist. He and his wife, Pat Shipman, provided a very readable story of the dig in *The Wisdom of Bones*.

Since fossils are mineralised, they are delicate and difficult to spot. Fossil hunting is an art for the tenacious, keen-eyed and well-trained. Once found, the fossil must be liberated from its substrate with great care. The team concentrated its searching in eroded gullies along the banks of the river, where fossils were most likely to be exposed. The team already had found many fossils of interest to museums and universities, but the dearest hope of its members was to find fossils that would fit into the jigsaw puzzle of human evolution.

The team actually was resting in camp, but one of its Kenyan members, Kamoya Kimeu, was restless. He wandered off to a small hill on the opposite bank of the river. There Kamoya found a small fossil (about 2 x 4 cm) that he recognised as the frontal bone of the thick skull of *Homo erectus,* one of our predecessors.

Kamoya Kimeu's find sparked a major excavation which continued over several annual working seasons into 1988. Some 1500 cubic yards of earth and rocks were painstakingly removed by hand and sifted. The results were of great importance. The most complete *Homo* skeleton ever had been discovered, more complete than the amazing find of Lucy. Sixty-seven fossil bones were found, representing all bones in the body except for the hands and feet. The skeleton was confirmed to be that of *Homo erectus*, a male, equivalent in dental development to a modern 11-year-old. Alan Walker called him Nariokotome Boy, but in other texts the term "Turkana Boy" may be used. Nariokotome Boy was tall for his age (1.61 metres). His maleness already had begun to appear in his facial characteristics. The boy's cranial capacity, projected into his adulthood, was estimated at 0.91 litres. Nariokotome Boy had lived approximately 1.53 $\pm$ 0.05 million years ago.

Exhaustive studies of the Nariokotome Boy fossils have followed, using established and innovative forensic and comparative techniques by a whole team of experts whom Alan Walker consulted. From these, Alan Walker drew a compassionate picture of this young *Homo erectus.*

The average dimensions of adult *Homo erectus* are

1.71 metres in height, 58 kilograms in weight, and 0.91 litres cranial capacity, so the boy was an average representative of his species. His brain was only two-thirds that of a modern human in terms of cranial capacity. He had the height of a human 15-year-old with the brain size of a human one-year-old. But although the boy may have looked rather like a human, he probably did not act like a human. Based on the robustness of the boy's femur, Alan Walker calculated that the boy was very strong, compared with modern human beings, and lanky as an adaptation to the tropics. Indeed, Alan Walker called him "hyper-tropical".

Unlike the Australopithecine who had long, sloping faces with no appreciable noses, perhaps reflecting their arboreal ancestors whose unhampered stereoscopic vision was critical for moving in trees, Nariokotome Boy had a definite nose. Indeed, the side maxillary bones and upper nasal bones of his face suggested that his nose was quite pronounced.

Although his brain was bigger than *Homo habilis*, Nariokotome Boy's encephalisation quotient was about the same. The boy had a much lower encephalisation quotient than we do, but it should be remembered that *Homo erectus* survived from two million years ago to about 200,000 years ago (some think until even 50,000 years ago), an achievement that our own species will do well to better.

Nariokotome Boy had narrow hips relative to us and to the Neandertal. These would have aided his locomotion and given him a swinging stride, which undoubtedly was an important survival trait, but it does raise the question of neoteny mentioned above. Alan Walker discussed this at length, calculating what the boy's internal pelvic circumference, the birth canal, would have been, had he been an adult female, and how big a newborn *Homo erectus* head would be. He concluded that the human pattern, whereby the brain continues to grow at fetal rates after birth, was already evolving in *Homo erectus* and *Homo habilis*. Since their brains are comparatively small, perhaps the implications of neoteny would not be as dramatic as they are with us but, nonetheless, because of the consequent period of infant dependency, it can be inferred that *Homo erectus* was social and cooperative within its own group.

Since high-quality protein was needed to feed the mothers suckling the infant *Homo erectus* with their developing brains, Alan Walker made a second inference, that they had developed a predatory habit. For him, this explained the rapid spread of *Homo erectus*, soon after its evolution as a species, as it followed the migrating herds it fed upon, within Africa and east to Asia and, about one million years ago, through the Middle East to the Caucasus and Eurasia. Their populations eventually extended as far as China, Java, north-western Africa and western Europe. He did not think that population pressures were sufficient to force migrations of *Homo erectus*. Surprisingly, *Homo erectus* did not make much advance in tool-making and there is thus a question as to how additional meat was obtained. There is the suggestion that the relatively short gastrointestinal tract of a carnivore, which *Homo erectus* was guessed to have, may be economical of energy and so compensate for the protein demands of braininess. *Homo erectus* may have been instinctively migratory, with an itch to travel. An alternative scenario will be discussed shortly.

It has already been mentioned that the conical shape of Lucy the Australopithecine's rib cage, precluded the controlled breathing necessary for speech. Alan Walker noticed a related speech impediment in the

Nariokotome Boy. It was the size of the boy's vertebral canal, which was half the diameter of a modern human being's, especially in the thoracic (the ribs) section. The spinal cord of nerve tissue must therefore also have been thin. The size of the brain and the vertebral canal are linked because the latter carries information to and from the brain. He surmised that the boy must have been comparatively unaware. The narrow thoracic vertebral canal also indicated that there was insufficient nerve supply, to the muscles between the ribs, to control breathing in order to speak words. This facility in human beings is related to the nervous pathways in the thoracic spinal cord. Alan Walker consulted authorities on the evolution of proto-languages and the effect of genes on speech. He was disappointed to conclude that Nariokotome Boy and, by extrapolation, all his ilk, were unable to speak as we do.

An inability to speak does not mean an inability to think. *Homo erectus* were sufficiently competent to survive and thrive for over a million years. The species probably had evolved an ability to think, even if it seems safe to say that none of its members could realistically aspire to be an orator.

Homo erectus were footloose, for they spread out of Africa on two great migrations. In the next chapter we shall explore whether this restlessness was an exaptation, and follow them on their journeys.

Chapter Five - Following Their Noses

Moving north, the émigrés
Fed upon the herds that graz'd;
With a nose for hamburgers
They became Heidel-burghers.

This chapter begins in company with *Homo erectus* as they tramped around their world, which often was very cold. Some of the predators with which they had to deal were truly awesome. However, *Homo erectus* was powerful and well adapted for striding confidently. Cave dwelling must have remained a central feature of their existence. As mentioned, they existed from about two million years ago to about 200,000 years ago or later. Clive Gamble (*Timewalkers*) and Robin McKie (*ape•man*) are the main points of reference in the following discussion.

There were most likely three major migrations out of Africa: 1.7 million years ago; 840,000 to 420,000 years ago; and 150,000 to 80,000 years ago, according to Alan Templeton, as cited by Richard Dawkins in *The Ancestor's Tale*. My interpretation is that two migrations involved *Homo erectus*. The third involved a successor of *Homo erectus*, *Homo heidelbergensis*.

However, not all authorities differentiate between the two species, while others add in other species. It is simpler to think of *Homo erectus* being the forerunner of both the Neandertal and *Homo sapiens*, but I have chosen to accept the current opinion that *Homo heidelbergensis* should be mentioned.

The three migrations comprised Alan Templeton's Out of Africa Again and Again theory. Low sea levels and resultant land bridges assisted migration by our own species, *Homo sapiens*, east around the Indian Ocean, according to Spencer Wells, who leads the worldwide Genographic Project and wrote *The Journey of Man*, which is an important reference later in this book. Low sea levels must have assisted earlier migrations by other *Homo* species as well. Routes would not have been terminally hampered by present geographic challenges such as the English Channel, the Mediterranean Sea, the Red Sea or the Arabian/ Persian Gulf, because of low sea levels. Robin McKie pointed out that the distance from Africa to Java could have been covered in 25,000 years, even if *Homo erectus* groups moved only at the rate of 16 kilometres per generation.

Robin McKie, in his wrap-up of prevailing thought on human evolution for the BBC2 television series *ape•man*, described how *Homo erectus* actually reached Java by 1.8 million years ago; in other words, soon after it evolved. In doing so, the Javanese variants seem to have isolated themselves because they did not appear to have the newer tools that their African cousins later developed.

There is no real need for us to proceed further on this first tramp, nor to hike to Georgia or China, where *Homo erectus* fossils dated to 1.8 million years also have been found. The connection between this very old period of movement and the present has not yet been clarified.

For the sake of simplicity, we shall therefore concentrate on the first "Again" of Alan Templeton's theory, or what Richard Dawkins suggested might be called the Middle Out of Africa emigration.

Out of Africa Again

Though the émigrés could have had no purposeful plan in mind, they did have a lot of time on their hands. The world must have been a bustling place, as species other than *Homo* moved restlessly as well, presumably in an integrated way, with predators/parasites driving/following prey and climatic factors impacting on all. The movements can be imagined as organic and dynamic, occurring in space and time, even though *Homo erectus* groups may have seemed to meander rather than migrate; climates and sea levels may have changed imperceptibly; and individuals within groups may have been subject to the effects of natural selection, and gene flow to and from other groups. I have borrowed Clive Gamble's metaphor, to help make sense of it all: timewalkers. In *Timewalkers* he argued that the importance of the prehistory of human colonisation has been overlooked by most writers. He considered that the tendency to date human civilisation from only the advent of agriculture was to overlook a large part of human history. Richard Rudgley in *Lost Civilizations of the Stone Age* was more emphatic, "history" is an afterword to the Stone Age. On behalf of the dog, I agree heartily with them both, and especially with Clive Gamble's concept that our joint evolutionary process took place in both time and space. This book addresses the prehistory of dogs and people, which most books ignore by focusing on domestication and civilisation.

Clive Gamble rewrote prehistory along the lines of divisions of migrating species of hominids. His schedule is adapted below.

Years before present	Species divisions	Species	Places colonised
5 million to 1 million	Early hominids	Australopithecines, early *Homo*	Sub-Saharan Africa
1 million to 60,000	Ancients	*Homo erectus*, archaic *Homo sapiens*, early Neandertal, anatomically modern humans	Africa, mid-latitude Asia, Europe
60,000 to 40,000	Pioneers	classic Neandertal, archaic *Homo sapiens*, anatomically modern humans	continental Eurasia
50,000 to 10,000	Moderns	Anatomically modern humans	Australia, eastern Siberia, Pacific margins, Japan, Americas, unglaciated mountain chains
10,000 to 500			Arctic, Indian Ocean, deep Pacific, tropical rainforests, great sand deserts
500 to present			central and southern Atlantic Ocean
unoccupied			Antarctica

Clive Gamble's general argument of timewalking is a most useful way of looking at human evolution, and is good background for this book. But it is not necessary here to delve deeply into the nomenclature of specific groups of migrants, nor to adhere strictly to his schedule. For our purpose, which after all is to speculate rather broadly, *Homo erectus* may be regarded as typical Ancients; the Neandertal and archaic *Homo sapiens* as typical Pioneers; and anatomically modern humans as Moderns.

For Clive Gamble, the important issue was that *Homo erectus* and, to a much lesser extent, the Australopithecine, began to organise and socialise. He visualised a group of 25 to 50 individuals, sexually dimorphic (that is, females much smaller than males), with the breeding females and dependant infants at its core, under the supervision of an alpha male or males, and located at a safe sleeping place. Sub-adults and excess males explored and brought back information and resources to the core. The transfer of information was through grunts and gestures, along the lines of a honey-bee returning to its hive, and probably as theatrical. He described this interaction happening on open plains, but suitable caves must have been even more desirable. The variations of this basic model were many, but Clive Gamble's point was that both sexes needed to develop cooperative behaviour to reduce risk and begin the forming of society with all its complexities.

Drawing on the fossils in the Sterkfontein valley, referred to above in relation to Charles Kimberlin Brain, Clive Gamble imagined how the groups would have obtained a range of edible plants and, to a lesser extent, meat, and how they would, perhaps, have shared the food within the group. He visualised power struggles, contests, intrigues, alliances and so on; the stuff of dynamic and increasingly complex society. Sub-adult males explored for territory and increased the range of the group and, since they were absent for longer periods as the range expanded, the intensity of socialisation increased to maintain coherence and alliances, and to encourage and digest the information that they brought home. Increased range meant that developing larger groups might be practicable and aid survival, adding to the selection pressure to migrate and explore around the core. Maintaining a cohesive society placed selection pressure on intelligence for organisation, but not necessarily for technological improvements in tools (for example). He considered that the adaptive behaviour of migration was an exaptation for colonisation because it honed the elements of omnivorous, mobile, dexterous and social behaviour, and the capacity to negotiate and navigate.

"Large brains, proper feet, nimble hands, fire, stone tools, and a range of feeding patterns were all assembled into a lifestyle package prior to any major expansion from Africa almost a million years ago," Clive Gamble wrote. The lifestyle package and expansion about one million years ago was due to pressure to extend *Homo erectus'* range for survival: the Ancients had begun to construct society as a "supra-organic niche". Their behaviour allowed eventual colonisation of the whole world by Moderns.

As we know from the skeleton of Nariokotome Boy, the Ancients were unlikely to be intellectually gifted – their encephalisation quotient was not significantly more than that of *Homo habilis*. They continued to use simple stone tools for millennia after boring millennia. Yet their social memories gave their societies a dimension of time as well as place, and they were bright enough to survive in equilibrium with their environment.

Some 730,000 to 780,000 years ago, *Homo erectus*

was caught up in a north-ward moving wave of migrating fauna which, as well as themselves, included the large spotted hyena and the lion, and, from the Middle East, wolves. The impetus seems to have been pulsations of climate change, but the method, in respect of *Homo*, was an integrated package of exapted behaviours. They entered an entirely different world to that of eastern Africa. As well as spreading to Europe, they also migrated to Asia, including Java and China, and within Africa spread south and north-west. In extreme climatic zones, these *Homo erectus* could not establish permanently. Until about 200,000 years ago, there is little archeological evidence of culture for the Ancients, no hearths, storage pits or architecture. Although stone tools were made they were simply used and discarded on site, and the Ancients moved on. In Clive Gamble's opinion, technology assisted *Homo erectus* rather than defining them.

As an aside, there is scant mention of birds in the *Homo* diet, perhaps because their light bones would not persist in the fossil record. However, it seems reasonable to assume *Homo* would have been cunning enough to set up hides, and ambush migrating water birds that flocked to lakes and streams. These were brought down with throwing sticks and specially shaped stones. In fact, *Homo erectus* invented the stone hand axe, called Acheulean because the first one to be described was found at Saint Acheul in France. The axe has since been found from South Africa to Europe, from the Mediterranean to India and Indonesia. It was in use for a million years. The axe was a teardrop of stone, usually about 15 centimetres long and about two kilograms in weight. It was generally assumed to be used for butchering carcasses and smashing bones for marrow.

However, Eileen O'Brien queried whether this tool

was used as an axe at all. Among other things she noted, is that its teardrop shape always gave it an "eccentric centre of gravity" and she considered that this improved the accuracy of the weapon, if it was thrown in the same way as a discus. She noted the profusion of hand axes found along watercourses and assumed this is because animals tend to congregate there. She visualised *Homo erectus* hunters raining axes down on to herbivores.

It seems just as likely it was used for bringing down waterfowl. The axe's eccentric centre of gravity would cause it to have an asymmetric flight path that birds in flight could not evade easily. The wooden boomerang is still used very effectively by hunters for this purpose.

My wife and I once were caught up in a small tribal fight in Port Moresby in Papua New Guinea. Stones of about one kilogram were the weapons being used since they were available at the roadside. They were thrown with astonishing force and calculated anger. These stones had not been shaped in any way, but were capable of fracturing legs, arms and skulls. The episode brought home to me that we should never dismiss the age of stone tools lightly. The use of paving stones in clashes, between protesters and police in the social revolts of the 1960s in Europe, taught authorities the wisdom of pre-emptive tarring of cobble-stoned streets, and the stone axes of Papua New Guinea are things of great beauty and balanced efficiency (although not to be compared with steel for practicality). One of my favourite tools is the stone mortar and pestle my wife gave me for grinding spices, and there remain many other uses for grindstones. Incidentally, we were not hurt in the fracas mentioned above, thanks to a Goilala man who warned us to return to the other side of the street: The police arrived and order was restored.

Stone hand axes, with shaped cutting edges and eccentric centres of gravity, must have been impressive weapons for offence and defence. Richard Rudgley describes the uniformity of the hand axe design as evidence for good communication between Ancients through the generations and throughout a wide geographic area: evidence of a social memory, abstract thought and the beginning of what he calls paleoscience.

There is considerable fossil information in mid-latitude Europe about the migrations of *Homo erectus*. These fossils are accessible and have been studied in depth. A short diversion is therefore warranted, with the help of Alan Turner who reviewed the literature and fossil finds from the period.

It was not until the middle Pleistocene, say one million years ago, that there was notable evidence of *Homo* migrations in Europe. Alan Turner assumed that the *Homo* were scavengers, mainly of the carcasses of large herbivores. Whatever their fowling skills were, at this time, scavenging was probably the chief modus operandi of the *Homo*. The important issues affecting the availability of meat to scavenge were the season, the habitat, size of the carcass and predator behaviour. Predator behaviour was quite critical to the outcome for a scavenger, because it determined what scraps were available and against whom the scavenger needed to compete for a share.

For the past million years, Europe was generally colder and drier than it is now. One million years ago, the fully glacial phase of the Pleistocene began, with the first stage being glacial and very cold through Eurasia. On the African continent habitats for animals began to open up into savannas. The Himalayan mountain chain rose faster, affecting climate and vegetation. In Europe *Homo erectus* probably relied mainly upon meat and animal fat for sustenance, because vegetable and marine foods were not available in sufficient quantities. Indeed *Homo* fossils do tend to be where fossils of terrestrial mammals are found.

In the European fossil record, there is a high diversity of fossils of herbivores and a plethora of associated fossils of carnivores, suggesting mouth-watering opportunities for our scavenging forebears. Alan Turner listed the herbivores and carnivores that were common, noting that at about 500,000 years ago there was a very marked shift in the nature and size of the populations. Herbivores included various ancestral species of rhinoceros, elephant, mammoth, elk, reindeer, giant deer, hippopotamus, and progenitors of cattle, sheep, goats, pigs, horses and gazelle. Carnivores were everywhere and were generally larger than those that still survive today. They included the sabre-toothed cats, the dirk-toothed cats, leopards, lions, bears, hyenas and wolves. Complexes of large herbivores and carnivores were ubiquitous through Eurasia, but the components of the complexes changed over time. The food resources for the *Homo erectus* thus changed according to the prey/predator complex, the season and the time they existed during the Pleistocene.

Their access to prey could be passive, as was more common in wooded areas where stealth was possible, or, in open areas, confrontational where, in the Mid-Pleistocene, three species of large hyena might be encountered, not to mention a number of canine species. Needless to say, *Homo erectus* had to contend with the owner of the kill, as well as trying on a daily basis to ensure that they were not the kill in question. Other scavengers, such as the large hyenas, must have been formidable competition for *Homo erectus*.

Given the climatic extremes compared with Africa and the competition from such dramatic carnivores, the migratory *Homo erectus* must have had a hard time persisting in Europe. Bones of *Homo erectus* and stone tools dating to 800,000 years ago have been found at Gran Dolina, near Burgo in Northern Spain, showing that the likes of Nariokotome Boy travelled there from Africa. However, they may not have been permanent inhabitants.

Homo heidelbergensis

About 500,000 years ago, the archaic forms of the large carnivores disappeared from the fossil record. Their disappearance was most likely due to the demise of the gigantic herbivores of the day, for reasons unknown. Their place was taken by smaller herbivores and a suite of carnivores more like those among which *Homo erectus* had evolved in eastern Africa: the leopards, lions and the aggressive spotted hyenas. Wolves also persisted. Whatever the changes were they must have affected *Homo erectus* also and exerted selection pressures for change. *Homo erectus* began to change, becoming a new species, called variously *Homo heidelbergensis*, or Archaic *Homo sapiens*, or even a trio of names, to include *Homo antecessor*.

The name of *Homo heidelbergensis* derived from a large, chinless jawbone 500,000 years old, found in a quarry near Heidelberg, Germany in 1907. Robin McKie described archeological finds in Boxgrove (in West Sussex, England, which at that time was joined to Europe by a land bridge), which show that *Homo erectus* had been transformed indeed. As *Homo heidelbergensis* it had become a cunning predator on large game using advanced tools and weapons, and showed signs of real intelligence. It could plan and organise hunts, and probably communicated in a sophisticated way. Recently, well-crafted spears 400,000 years old have been found near Heidelberg, at Schöningen. The Heidelbergs may have made simple dwellings.

It is clear that the Heidelbergs were brainy, with a braincase volume of 1.1 litres, close to the modern average. They remained tall and extremely strong and robust, like the Nariokotome Boy. Robin McKie saw their intelligence being of great assistance for survival at a time when climate fluctuations were extreme and frequent. However, little else is known about the Heidelbergs of that period, except, importantly, that their remains have been found at several sites in Africa and also in India and China, suggesting that impetus for change in *Homo erectus* was global. We shall revisit them in Africa later in this story.

Atapuercans and the Pit of Bones

A lot more is known about the next period we shall discuss, although the work is only 20 years old. Gran Dolina, near Burgo in northern Spain, has been mentioned already in relation to *Homo erectus* fossils and tools. Close by is Atapuerca Cavern. This is the site of the forbiddingly named Pit of Bones (La Sima de los Huesos) containing the remains of 32 *Homo*, which are 300,000 years old. The remains are not complete, in fact many pieces of the bodies are missing and there is evidence of cannibalism. Nonetheless, the Pit is a treasure trove of information. The Pit itself is deep and narrow, and its depths are virtually airless. Its discovery and investigation are testaments to the tenacity and bravery of the team of Juan Luis Arsuaga Ferreras, himself one of the first explorers of the Pit.

No tools have been found in the Pit, therefore it is most likely the bodies (mostly those of adolescents) were flung into it by perpetrators unknown.

The bodies in the Pit show that the Atapuercans were tall and sturdy, had brain cases of varying sizes, had heavy brow ridges and noticeably big noses. They looked very different from modern humans, wrote Juan Luis Arsuaga Ferreras, referring to a model based on a well-preserved skull. Robin McKie commented that the people of La Sima were tall, like the Heidelbergs, but their anatomy was different in some respects. For example, the middle of their faces projected strikingly. They must have had large, prominent noses, along the lines of the Neandertal nose, to be discussed shortly. Robin McKie assumed their large nose was an adaptation to the cold climate, to warm inhaled air before it reached the area of the brain. Their tallness led Robin McKie to comment that their physiques had not yet adapted for cold climates by becoming stocky.

Winning by a Nose

Robin McKie's comment on the Atapuercan nose begs me to pose the question: If the big nose is an adaptation of *Homo erectus* descendants to the cold, and so is a stocky physique, how can the first happen and not the latter in the Atapuercans, after the passage of so much time since the arrival of *Homo erectus* from Africa?

A far more parsimonious explanation is that the Atapuercans were further evidence that *Homo erectus* and its descendants, including the Neandertal, to whom we shall be introduced by Marcellin Boule in a few pages, obtained survival benefits from a good sense of smell. Like *Homo erectus* they were on the path to becoming nosier as well as brainier.

Chapter Six - Neandertal

Proof of Nature's acumen
Were Neandertal wo/men;
Brawn and prodigious senses,
Beefed up their defences.

The Pit of Bones was a sobering place to stop and reflect. However, we can now hurry on, armed with the thought that *Homo heidelbergensis* had continued its forebears' propensity for nosiness. The discussion in this chapter owes much to Christopher Stringer and Robin McKie, who wrote *African Exodus*.

Homo heidelbergensis individuals were smart, they had enhanced intelligence as evidenced by their weapons and social organisation. The Heidelbergs most likely were deft spear throwers, if we recall the well-crafted spears found at Schöningen. They were becoming brainier. This locked them further into longer periods of infant dependency and all the complexities that that entailed. Safe places for the core families remained essential. These almost certainly would be caves. Caves may have been hotly contested by other Heidelbergs and other cave-dwelling species. The Heidelbergs had inherited a strategy for migration from *Homo erectus*, but rising sea levels reduced the amount of territory they could exploit.

As *Homo heidelbergensis* populations reached survival limits there must have been a gradual increase in naturally selective pressures for alternative evolutionary strategies. The effects of these pressures are of particular popular interest, since the issue is the direction our own evolution has taken. I have drawn on stories in *Archaeology* (Mark Rose), *Scientific American* (Kate Wong) and *National Geographic News* (Elizabeth Svoboda) for the discussion following. The consensus seems to be that *Homo neanderthalensis* was one outcome of these pressures. Recent mitochondrial deoxyribonucleic acid (mtDNA) analysis of tissue, amazingly extracted from a 40-50,000-year-old Neandertal humerus by Svante Pääbo and colleagues, shows that Neandertal are a separate species to *Homo sapiens*, although we share a common ancestor with them. The same analysis shows that their speciation occurred about 550,000 to 690,000 years ago. More recent analysis of nuclear DNA by James Noonan and colleagues has dated the most recent common ancestor of Neandertal and people at about 400,000 years ago. The Svante Pääbo team continues working to sequence the entire Neandertal genome and has found evidence of mingling of genes between Neandertal and human beings, perhaps in the Middle East, and perhaps 45,000 to 80,000 years ago.

So, four to five hundred thousand years ago, the stocky, broad-hipped, brainy, nosey, brawny, in-your-face, belt-and-braces Neandertal came into being, finely tuned for its environment by the power of natural selection.

Belt and Braces

The Neandertal had an even larger brain than modern human beings (cranial volumes of 1.2 to 1.75 litres) and so was locked further into neotenic development. This is borne out by analysis of Neandertal tooth enamel, which shows similar growth patterns to modern children, but there is also a recent suggestion that the Neandertal children may have developed more quickly than equivalent modern children. In shape, their brain was flatter at the top, bulged more at the sides and back, and was smaller at the front than the human brain. Christopher Stringer and Robin McKie concluded that the Neandertal strengths lay in observing things rather than in planning strategies. They had remarkable brow ridges, which might have served to keep their hair out of their large eyes. They were bulky and squat in shape, the stockier individuals being found in colder north-west Europe. Gracile Neandertal lived in eastern Europe and western Asia. Their noses were phenomenally large. The Neandertal had massive faces, massive heads and massive bodies, with massive long bones as well, indicating they were very strong. They were likely to use brawn to solve their problems.

In 1992 in a cave near Galilee, Yoel Rak and colleagues uncovered the 60,000-year-old grave of a Neandertal infant some 10 months of age. The jawbone of a red deer had been placed over the child's pelvis, suggesting a funeral offering. Most striking, however, was the alien appearance of its skull. The child had no chin. The hole at the base of the skull (the occipital foramen), through which the spinal cord passes, was highly elongated instead of round, and there was evidence that the ligament and muscles from the skull to the inside of the lower jawbone must already have been very well developed. This suggested a very powerful bite and chew. These signs in an infant indicated that the adult Neandertal were very different to modern human beings.

They were incredibly strong by modern human standards. Australian anthropologist Peter McAllister has written an amusing book, *Manthropology*, to highlight modern man's physical decline. From an analysis of her skeleton and cross-sections of her bones, he calculated that a Neandertal girl 1.53 metres tall and 80 kilograms in weight carried enough upper-body musculature to outwrestle a contemporary World Arm Wrestling champion, a Russian male much larger than she was. Modern human females carry only 50 per cent of a male's upper-body musculature, so Peter McAllister concluded that the World Arm Wrestling champion would have had no contest at all against a Neandertal male.

Neandertal Khan?

We can guess that the population from which the Neandertal arose was isolated geographically because this is often the way new species arise. Sufficient natural selection pressure was exerted on variations, including perhaps beneficial mutations in that population, to result in a new species. Once isolation of the population occurred, a disproportionate founder effect might have applied, especially if a dominant male and his descendants might have expropriated the females, or, if isolation was long enough, genetic drift might have been a factor. In either case, natural selection would determine the successful survivors, whom we shall soon describe in some detail.

It seems unlikely that the Atapuercans could have been the source of the Neandertal. The skeletons in the Pit of Bones are only 300,000 years old. They post-date the Neandertal and were not stocky. The stocky figures of the Neandertal suggest they were well adapted to cold climates. This is a reason to think that the isolated population from which they originated was in a cold climate. Neandertal nuclear DNA indicates the speciation event was 400,000 years ago, yet the first evidence of Neandertal in Europe, regarded as their stronghold, is not until 200,000 years ago, and their presence in the Levant is only from about 100,000 years ago.

Perhaps the Neandertal arose in the east, in the cold middle latitudes and drifted westward north of the Himalayas, perhaps even pushed along by that rising, mighty mountain chain. Perhaps they eventually spread into western Europe, to reach an impasse in the Iberian peninsula. Perhaps shortages of caves got them on the move again, east and south into the Levant, there to meet up with their African cousins, who had evolved from *Homo erectus* into *Homo heidelbergensis*. If this seems simplistic, consider Spencer Wells' account of human Y chromosome analysis in relation to *Homo sapiens* migrations (Y chromosomes will be discussed more fully shortly). The modern human beings who entered Europe and out-competed the Neandertal came from the east, not directly from Africa. If we could do it, why could not the powerful, stocky Neandertal arrive from the east and out-compete the Heidelbergs in the higher latitudes?

According to Erik Trinkaus and Pat Shipman, the Neandertal displayed elements of early modern human behaviour: they had large complex brains, buried their dead (but Christopher Stringer thinks that later Neandertal may have learnt this practice from modern humans with whom they cohabited in the Levant), cared for the injured and wore ornaments. Some of these claims are controversial. The behaviour of the European Neandertal was nonmodern. Nonetheless they may have been impressive athletes, as the Neandertal had very well developed shoulder muscles and deep chests. They too may have excelled in the use of weapons. Having to work at close quarters with very large prey may account for the many healed breakages observed in their bones. When scavenging, Neandertal would have had to confront the aggressive spotted hyena, not to mention the leopard, lion and wolf. Life was risky for them. Healed fractures show they had a social conscience and looked after one another. They must have communicated well in some form of language (but not speech, to be explained shortly).

All in all, a Neandertal was a formidable opponent with which early humans had to contend. They have been called ultra-human. They were the logically explicable outcome of natural selection. They were a very successful species, dominating a limited area for 300,000 years until their extinction less than 30,000 years ago when they ran out of time, soon after *Homo sapiens* arrived in Europe.

I shall now move to a detailed discussion of why these ultra-humans ran out of time, but to conclude this section I shall give you a hint, by quoting some of Colin Groves' words in the David Paterson film *The Secret Life of the Dog*.

Colin Groves: "Neandertal and sapiens were about equally advanced ... they had similar stone tools ... they had similar modes of life. Neandertal buried their dead ... they used fire ... they presumably took care of their old people because we have found some buried skeletons of people who were extremely aged ... they were real human beings. The brain sizes of the Neandertal and the earliest *Homo sapiens* were about the same … both are about 1500 cubic centimetres, which is larger than the mean size of any living people … they were overlapping from about 120,000 to 30,000 years ago and it was going to take something quite special to dislodge them. Some people envisage warfare – *Homo sapiens* strolling into Europe, knocking the Neandertal on the head. I don't think anything of the kind … in fact, the Neandertal faded out because the sapiens were doing something better … were doing the same sort of thing, just that little bit better … because they had a companion to do it with."

I take Colin Groves' comment a little further: *Homo sapiens* were doing things better because the Neandertal did not have a companion who was part of their phenotype. As a result, the Neandertal were never able to speak in a staccato volley of words. And that made the fatal difference.

Ultra-Humans

When the Neandertal were thought to be the direct ancestors of human beings, most researchers were tactful in their comments about them. Not so Marcellin Boule, the French anthropologist who early described fossils of the species named *Homo neanderthalensis*. Marcellin Boule was accused of bias in his assessment of the Neandertal skeleton called the Old Man of Chappelle. The Old Man's skull was discovered in a small cave near Chappelle-aux-Saints, France in 1908 and is about 40,000 years old. Marcellin Boule's description is useful in this book.

Concerning his alleged bias, it must be said that Marcellin Boule was one of the few who was not sucked in by the Piltdown Hoax. The Piltdown Hoax involved the fabrication of the "missing link" in human evolution. A modern skull and a simian jaw, suitably disguised, were buried together and found in 1911 in a gravel bed at Piltdown in Sussex, England. The hoax was successful, largely because the find met English expectations that the first human being would be British. The story is very well known. It is a rather uninteresting account of human frailties that held back the study of human origins for 25 years. It will not be discussed further except to note that, when a tooth of *Homo heidelbergensis* was found at Boxgrove, in England, in 1995, the historical society English Heritage was very excited that the earliest Englishman had been found!

Marcellin Boule described the Old Man's skull as follows: "The nose, separated from the forehead by a deep depression, is short and very broad; by a prolongation of the malar bones, the upper jaw forms a kind of muzzle ... the maxillaries stand out as a continuation of the zygomatic arches, and accentuate the muzzle-like form of the face ... orbits are widely separated and relatively large, half as great again as modern man of similar brain capacity ... this fossil man, which in so many of his characters approaches the apes more than any other man, is nevertheless so widely divergent from them as regards his nasal region, that instead of being simian in this respect, he might be looked upon as ultra-human." A Neandertal child's skull from La Quina also showed the muzzle-like appearance, according to Marcellin Boule, with immense rounded orbits and broad nose.

One can see how confronting it might be to use the word "muzzle" in relation to a possible forebear. Yoel Rak called it a "snout". Christopher Stringer gives us another form of words that is less confronting, but which still makes the point. In *African Exodus*, written with Robin McKie, he wrote that the most remarkable organ the Neandertal possessed (as far as is known, within the limits of fossil evidence) was its nose, which was "phenomenal". It was both wide and projecting, sticking out horizontally between the eyes and accentuated by sweeping cheekbones (maxilla). The Neandertal skull had enormous nasal apertures and cavernous sinuses.

Christopher Stringer ponders the question of the Neandertal face: "But what evolutionary advantage could there have been in having a protuberance like the Tower of Lebanon? A heightened sense of smell, perhaps? Well, possibly, though such olfactory powers would have bucked the general trend of primate evolution which has de-emphasised the sense of smell, in over the past 40 million years. In any case, most mammals with such a sense usually have flat noses with moist tips, like dogs – but unlike Neandertals."

Christopher Stringer does not enlarge on why he thinks Neandertal had dry noses, but regarding nose size, he was influenced by Erik Trinkaus and Pat Shipman, who are leading authorities on the Neandertal. They suggested that the very big noses of the Neandertal were to warm up the Ice Age air they inhaled. This is in line with their proposition that the Neandertal depended upon the biological processes of evolution rather than cultural evolution, and these processes locked them into massive bodies. In opposition were the views of Arthur Jelinek and Clive Gamble, who considered that conclusions about the functions of the markedly projecting faces, large anterior teeth, large nasal apertures and large orbits of the western European Neandertal could be premature, since there is evidence of survival of *Homo* in cold-climate Europe prior to the Neandertal, and also because modern humans have populated cold climates for generations without developing extreme anatomies.

The American Academy of Sciences commissioned Jay Matternes to reconstruct a Neandertal face from a skull about 46,000 years old from the Shanidar cave in northern Iraq. The skull the Academy used had heavy brow ridges and a projecting upper jaw. Soft structures such as olfactory tissues (which include olfactory membranes supported by cartilaginous and light turbinate bones) did not survive in the fossil record, of course. Jay Matternes had to rely upon evidence of bony ridges for muscle attachment to guess the shape of overlying structures. His reconstruction showed the Neandertal with a large nasal and maxillary area (and a benign, likeable, slightly bemused expression). The matter was addressed again by a team from the National Geographic Society who used a computer to depict a Neandertal face: "... so massive are the Neandertal crania that the model's eyes stretched noticeably – they had to be redrawn on the screen manually ... some experts believe Neandertal noses were even bigger than the computer's reconstructions." The widely spaced orbits of the Neandertal presumably were an adaptation of a bipedal animal to a very large nose or muzzle. With a muzzle blocking the vision of the Neandertal, manipulative skills may not have developed as well as these did in us. This could have interfered with fine tasks and accurate throwing of spears, for example. In a reconstruction of a four-year-old Neandertal child's head and face, shown in Christopher Stringer and Peter Andrew's *The Complete World of Human Evolution*, the muzzle is conjectured to be quite soft in outline, although the chin is absent. This child had an estimated brain volume of an amazing 1.4 litres. The child was depicted as cute and personable.

While a Neandertal juvenile might have softened features, it seems likely from the descriptions above that the Neandertal facial characteristics differed significantly from human beings'.

Recently Mati Milstein reported in *National Geographic News* that William Hylander and Yoel Rak noted that the Neandertal had a noticeable gap between the back molar teeth and the vertical arm of the lower jawbone. They presented findings that Neandertal could open their mouths very wide. It seems unlikely that Neandertal ever suffered from impacted wisdom teeth. Their ability to open their mouths wide may have helped them to "taste the air", adding to their olfactory prowess, if their Jacobson's organs were in working order. This organ, also called the vomeronasal organ, is located at the back of the oral and nasal cavities, in the soft mucosal tissue near the rearwards end of the nasal septum that divides the nostrils.

The organ is lined with receptor cells, which make it useful in many animals for detecting chemicals in the air. In mammals it serves to aid olfaction, and particularly aids the detection of pheromones (chemical signals) from females who are receptive to mating. In snakes the vomeronasal organ actually is the organ of smell, the snake's flicking tongue sampling air particles and carrying them back to the organ, to be "tasted". The vomeronasal organ itself is a thin tube, usually paired, and usually with a blind end and two open ends. In modern humans it is detectable in the embryo, but in the adult is merely a small pit. Although only a vestige of its former self, the tissue comprising the vomeronasal organ has been shown to be physiologically responsive to human steroids and may have an effect on the release of reproductive hormones.

The vomeronasal organ is well developed in dogs and a number of farm animals. Anyone who has seen "tonguing" male dogs following a female dog in estrus ("heat") will have noticed their gaping mouths and lolling tongues, suggestive of utter exhaustion. It is much more likely that they are in thrall to the imperatives of biology, as pheromones communicate a mutually beneficial message from the female to the males.

The argument of this book is that the most parsimonious explanation for the Neandertal muzzles is that the muzzles evolved to enhance their sense of smell, as well as to support large jaws with big, strong teeth. The Neandertal were further advanced along the same trajectory of evolution as that of Nariokotome Boy and the Atapuercans. In this respect, as Christopher Stringer noted, it is the human being who is exceptional in lacking a well-developed sense of smell. Erik Trinkaus was quoted (*Science Daily*, 8 September 2006, webpage): "If we want to better understand human evolution, we should be asking why Modern Humans are so unusual, not why the Neandertal are divergent. Modern Humans, for example, are the only people who lack brow ridges. We are the only ones who have seriously shortened faces. We are the only ones with very reduced internal nasal cavities. We also have a number of detailed features of the limb skeleton which are unique."

Thank you, Erik Trinkaus. His questions and more are addressed in this book. To take the argument further, the next chapter deals with the limited ability which Neandertal had for speech. They could communicate in tongues, but not in words, because they had a muzzle.

Chapter Seven - The Anatomy for Speech

Eloquence is intricate:
Voice, tongue, teeth, lips must partake,
Before can be uttered,
That fine, felicitous Word.

Animals communicate effectively within specific groups in very many ways and this makes the discussion of language as communication a rather slippery thing. Communication may even be unconscious as hypothesised by Rupert Sheldrake in *The Presence of the Past*. He suggested that behavioural information can be transmitted by the resonance of morphic fields between members of a species, and he organised formal experiments to study whether morphic fields can transmit information between people and other animals, especially the dog.

Even when the discussion is focused on the communication of ideas or moods, usually within a species, language is a very broad concept. The Black-faced Cuckoo Shrike perching on our powerline has language: It raises its wing to signal something deep and meaningful to its kith and kin, although the gesture just looks quaint to me.

On the matter of quaintness, we have already mentioned the probable honey-bee communication of our early ancestors: It is not difficult to imagine these theatrics developing into miming and sign language. Body language is a way of communicating basic ideas within a species, as with tail flashes in a herd of antelope, or lip smacking and grimaces among chimpanzees. This kind of physical communication can extend between species. Chimpanzees can be taught sign language and communicate their wants to their keepers.

Dogs and people soon learn the body language of each other. We can communicate quite well. For example, Toby our dog has taught me to respond to his body language sufficient for him to live a fulfilling and happy life, despite human constraints. The ideas he communicates are: Will you wake up and let me out (for a walk with the neighbour); is that breakfast/lunch?!; OMG! Is that the postman AGAIN!!!; is it time for dinner?; let's go for a walk; I am sleepy – have you set up my bed? With words I communicate to him the ideas of sit; come; stay; be quiet! and so on with some success, although he verges on the defiantly obtuse sometimes. He can read our body language for going out and adopts a dejected mien, which changes instantly to unfettered joy when he is told that he can come too: His tail whirls in circular fashion. We have reached a happy equilibrium in communication that is sufficient for our needs.

Many animals vocalise to communicate and convey categories of information. Basic concepts such as aggression, yearning, food, danger, mothering and so on are transmitted by wind sounds (elephants also let their intestines do the talking).

The discussion here is about a particular form of vocalisation: Spoken language in *Homo*, especially about speaking words.

Speech is not the be-all and end-all of language. For example, I imagine that a dolphin's sonar could assess the state of my liver and negate the need for it to ask me how I am. Farley Mowat in *Never Cry Wolf* describes how he scent marked around his cabin to warn his study wolves not to trespass. All that he required to communicate with wild wolves was copious draughts of water and a sense of humour.

But speech is very creative because it uses words to build and transmit/receive more complicated concepts. It is a unique language skill that really does differentiate us among other animals. Speech is a part of language. It is the ability to enunciate words, understand them, make them up and think about them.

Speech was attributed to a gene in *Homo sapiens*, perhaps a mutation, which created, somewhat miraculously, a universal grammar. But a far more convincing proposition is that speech is an evolved trait in *Homo* and can be explained by Charles Darwin's theory of natural selection. It is thanks mainly to Lloyd DuBrul (*Evolution of the Speech Apparatus*), Philip Lieberman (*The Biology and Evolution of Language*) and the recent ideas of Peter MacNeilage (*The Origin of Speech*) and Robin Dunbar (*Grooming, Gossip, and the Evolution of Language*) that I am able to carry the argument further in this section.

How would the theory of natural selection explain the evolution of speech? Robin Dunbar noted that grooming is primate behaviour that bonds groups. As the number of individuals in the group increases so does grooming time, until a limit of about a third of activity time is spent in grooming behaviour. Grooming is both pleasurable physical sensation and social intercourse. Larger groups aid survival, but require increase in brain size (the neocortex) in individuals as interactions become more complex. Spoken language evolved to extend the effects of grooming beyond physical contact and thus facilitate the social viability of larger groups. Our brains can now handle social groups of up to about 150 individuals. *Homo* brains may have been big enough 250,000 years ago to manage stable social groups as large as 120 to 130 individuals, but the making and later trading of stone tools before this suggests a developing capacity for language. Since grooming is most intense at the core of the group where females are located, it is likely that spoken language evolved first among females.

Peter MacNeilage accepted the importance of grooming in the evolution of speech. I shall try to condense how he sees speech evolving. Peter MacNeilage argued that the structures adapted for ingestion of food are exaptations for speech. Chewing was an exaptation for mandibular (jaw) cyclicity. Lip smacking and facial grimaces, useful for visuofacial communication, led to vibrations of the mandible, which eventually become paired with the vibration of the vocal folds (voicing), creating the first syllables. Syllables are the necessary result of the way vocal folds operate. The tighter they flex, the greater is the tendency for them to return to the relaxed position of rest. Voicing thus is necessarily staccato or syllabic. Since these sounds were very simple and could be perceived by another *Homo*, a two-staged process began whereby forms framed content and led to perceivable speech, which may initially have been like the babble of babies. Motor activity refined from the miming mentioned above in relation to our early ancestors, may have been an exaptation for "spitting out" the first simple words. Framed content allowed longer utterances as areas in the brain evolved capacity to pair simple frame structures with concepts. Peter MacNeilage noted that Broca's area in the brain is associated with speech, eating and probably visuofacial communication as well. Broca's area will be discussed shortly.

The theory of natural selection can explain that the ability to speak depends upon the evolution of many structures in the body that produce and perceive words. Anatomy and society are aspects of this ability. These are discussed below and in subsequent chapters, to show that the evolution of human speech also required an extended phenotype in which to occur.

Lost for Words

The review of Steven Pinker (*The Language Instinct*) also informs the discussion in this section. In relation to our ancestors, Steven Pinker thought that, on balance, Lucy the Australopithecine had language, given her likely social life. He referred to internal casts of the fossil cranium of one of her successors, *Homo habilis* (Handyman), which suggested that those parts of the left hemisphere of the brain that contain Broca's and Wernicke's areas were present, so Handyman probably had language too.

Broca's area was named for Paul Broca, a French anatomist who, in 1861, discovered an area near the lateral fissure of the left cerebral hemisphere that controlled the mechanisms of speech – the gestures of the tongue and other organs in the human head. A decade later, Carl Wernicke, a German neurologist, discovered an associated area that controlled the production and understanding of words. It was located on the other side of the lateral fissure. These two areas are connected by a loop of nerve tissue running around the lateral fissure. The area and the loop would not of course leave any signs in a cranial cast from a fossil skull, although the fissure could. The loop is also found in deaf people who use sign language, so it is a step removed from heard or spoken language. Language functions include a third area, in the temporal cortex of the brain, which was discovered in the 1960-70s by the American neurologist Norman Geschwind. The resultant Geschwind-Wernicke model was that each aspect of language is managed by distinct interconnected modules in the brain.

It might be noted that other animals, such as the dog, have well-developed lateral fissures in their left hemispheres. Many animals need to communicate with their ilk by accessing, processing, understanding and reacting to sounds (and other signals). Therefore, one could expect that the Geschwind-Wernicke model would have a long and not specific evolutionary history.

The spoken word, that is, speech, is the focus of this book, rather than communication *per se*. In this book, the Neandertal lack of facility with words is argued as a factor determining whether they survived or not, once *Homo sapiens* arrived on the scene. In essence, whether the felicitous Word proved mightier than blunt Brawn. Richard Rudgley, in *Lost Civilizations of the Stone Age*, points out that the Neandertal must have been able to communicate quite well to bury and venerate their dead, set broken bones, amputate limbs and trade stone tools; and they almost certainly had forms of symbolic art.

But, could the Neandertal speak in words? Steven Pinker pointed out that, even with few vowels, language can be quite expressive. If we forgive the Neandertal the need to use vowels, since these are complicated to produce and require anatomy which will be described shortly, our question could be rephrased: "Cld th Nndtl spk?" A writer of Hebrew, a language with few written vowels, or a patient and perceptive speaker of English might reply: "Sort of." And if the Neandertal tended to slur their consonants because of their big mouths and loose tongues, the question would be: "Cccll hhh lll ssskkk?" Would the answer again be: "Sort of"? Of course it would! The Neandertal could speak. The Neandertal had many elements of awakening human behaviour inherited from its migratory *Homo erectus* and Heidelberg ancestors. Neandertal could communicate well with each other. The question should have been, "How well could the Neandertal speak?"

Not as well as we can, and, with the gift of Darwinian hindsight, we can see that that failing was crucial. Speaking in tongues was not good enough.

Speaking words by human beings is no mean feat. In fact, it is truly amazing. One can imagine the Broca-Wernicke-Geschwind "microprocessors" running hot, burning up brain food: Peter MacNeilage points out that every second of speech requires an incredible 225 muscle actions involving the chest, larynx, throat, mouth and face. That is, one event every five milliseconds. The whole process is far too complex to be due to a mutant gene. Philip Lieberman considered that the process of natural selection appears to have produced a speech-perceiving system that is matched to the constraints of speech production, in us at any rate. And to enunciate clearly, the head must have the appropriate anatomy.

Head in a Whirl

To determine the appropriate anatomy for speech, the help of anatomist Lloyd DuBrul is enlisted. To investigate the evolution of the speech apparatus in human beings, he compared the anatomies of the heads of a progressive series of primates: a tree shrew, a lemur, an Old World monkey, a gibbon and a human being. His analysis was detailed and included views of the dissected heads from below and in section. To ensure that the comparisons of such very different animals were appropriate, he used a horizontal plane through the bottom of the eye socket to just above the ear canal to align each head with the others. This plane is called the Frankfurt plane and is based on a convention that it represents the way the human head is poised normally. A summary of Lloyd DuBrul's findings is given below.

The tree shrew is the most primitive of the group of primates, in the sense of lack of specialised development. It is not at all bipedal, its normal body axis is horizontal and its Frankfurt plane is more or less aligned with that axis. It has a long, narrow skull. The snout is in front and brain directly behind. The floor of its mouth is supported mainly by flat, wide anterior digastric muscles that insert into the mandibles (jaws) on each side and secondarily into the hyoid bone (to be explained presently). The spinal cord enters the skull through an opening, called the foramen magnum or the occipital foramen, positioned virtually right at the back of the skull. The neck of the tree shrew is thus more or less in line with its skull. (The dog is not a primate but, like the shrew, it needs a good sense of smell and catches prey with its teeth. Its head has evolved along a similar trajectory, with long jaws, loose tongue, large nasal area and large olfactory bulbs of the brain. Like the shrew its skull too is roughly in line with its neck in a horizontal plane).

The lemur is arboreal and has a propensity for sitting and standing, and generally moving through many planes. Its head appears less long and narrow than the shrew's and its face tends to "fall". The foramen magnum is slightly under the skull and not at the back as it was in the shrew. The neck therefore enters the head at a slight angle.

The Old World monkey is exclusively arboreal and very agile. Its posture is almost vertical when it leaps. Its skull is rounder than the lemur's and its face has dropped further down the skull. Its jaws are relatively shorter than the lemur's and its neck has moved further under the head as the foramen magnum moved forward.

The gibbon has the most habitually upright posture of the apes and, because it is a gifted swinger on branches (a brachiator), its Frankfurt plane is angled slightly above the horizontal, unlike ourselves whose Frankfurt plane is normally angled slightly downwards so we don't trip. The gibbon on the other hand needs to peer up to the point it is swinging to reach. The gibbon's skull is much more rounded than those animals so far described, and its foramen magnum has moved even further forward under the skull.

Human beings are terrestrial bipeds. Our skulls are rounded and our jaws shorter and wider – blunter – adding to the roundness of our heads. The foramen magnum has moved so far forward that its leading edge is virtually centred under the skull. The neck therefore may be said to support the head from almost directly underneath. The whole jaw is little more than half the length of the skull and is "abbreviated". The anterior digastric muscles do not form the floor of the mouth as in the tree shrew, but instead flare widely from the front to back. The hyoid bone hangs lower than in any of the other animals in the series. A description of the hyoid bone is given shortly.

The arrangement of the digastric muscles gave Lloyd DuBrul the impression that they had been progressively rearranged by natural selection in this series of species to disturb the stability of the hyoid bone as little as possible.

We need not discuss each case in detail, although we shall return to the human being shortly, but we can pause to reflect on what Lloyd DuBrul has shown. As an animal's posture becomes increasingly vertical to adapt better in its evolutionary niche, specific skull changes may occur, not necessarily due to the growth of the brain. The cranium becomes more domed, the face becomes angled downwards, the snout and jaws reduce in size and become relatively broader, and the foramen magnum migrates further forward under the skull, along with the supporting neck. Lloyd DuBrul also observed that the base of the skull (imagine the lower jaw is not there, for a moment) tends to flex or arch upwards, as though the fallen face is being tucked in. In human beings, as the lower borders of the shortening horizontal arms of the bottom jawbones flare outwards, a chin is formed where these two arms meet and fuse where the jawbones join. You can feel the flaring and your own chin easily with your fingers. The Neandertal had relatively large jaws and no chin.

Human Anatomy

The evolutionary paths of gibbons and human beings diverged many millions of years ago, but Lloyd DuBrul's description showed how natural selection operates and how rotation of the skull affects many structures. The discussion that now continues describes some of those structures, with particular reference to the human being.

The hyoid's name derives from the Greek hyoeides, meaning U-shaped. This bone attaches by ligaments to two thin, bony styloid (like a pen) processes that jut from the base of the skull on both sides, just under the ear canals. The hyoid bone might be imagined as the U-shaped part of a stethoscope when in use by a doctor. A network of muscles passes to and from the hyoid, attaching to the jaws and the skull, and, among other things, forming the floor of the mouth. The hyoid helps give purchase to the very muscular pedestal which is the base of the tongue, and, in human beings, swells to fill the mouth, contacting the wall of teeth at the front and sides. The larynx or voice box also is supported by the hyoid bone through a number of ligaments and muscles. As mentioned earlier, the digastric muscles have moved away from the hyoid, and the larynx therefore is not much affected by movements of the bottom jaw.

The larynx is a cartilaginous structure, not really like a box at all. It includes the entrance of the trachea (which carries air to and from the lungs); the epiglottis (a valve that involuntarily closes to prevent liquids, food and other foreign bodies entering the trachea); and the glottis, which is formed by folds of tissue on either side, which are the vocal folds. These vibrate with the passage of air and create the sounds that are the basis of vocalisation. Around the larynx is a soft-tissue chamber called the pharynx. This chamber begins at the back of the nose and mouth, and leads on to the esophagus, down which food and drink pass to the stomach.

The roof of the mouth is formed by the palate, which is hard at the front where it attaches to the internal upper jawbones of the skull, and soft and freely movable at the back, where it merges with the mucous membranes of the pharynx and rear nasal passages. In most animals with larynxes, including the human infant, the tip of the epiglottis fits under the edge of the soft palate and the rim of the tracheal cartilage fits against the walls of the pharynx such that there is a complete tube from the nose to the lungs. This means that breathing can continue even as the animal swallows. Hence the human infant can breathe while it suckles.

The situation changes as the child develops into an upright adult. The structures for breathing, swallowing and vocalisation in human beings are a soft integrated mass located securely by the hyoid bone but also relatively mobile. As the child begins to walk and gravity acts on the soft mass, the larynx slides downwards in relation to the neck. This creates a considerable gap between the epiglottis, the soft palate and the back of the nose. The gap can be imagined as a sound chamber. In the process, the larynx swivels such that its opening turns towards the back of the neck (nearly at right angles to the Frankfurt plane) and faces into the food-carrying part of the pharynx leading to the esophagus. This is why adult human beings quite frequently choke on food and drink, when passing food particles trigger the epiglottis into spasm.

Choking is a significant cause of death in human beings and would be naturally selected against, except that, as Lloyd DuBrul pointed out, our quirky anatomy liberated us to be a talking animal: "With the retreat of the larynx from the encroaching tongue, a great gap is opened between the epiglottis and soft palate. Entirely new operations are possible. Man is the first animal able to close off the nasal tubes from the rest of the airway completely, easily, speedily, and habitually. The soft palate acts as a valve. It shunts noisy air blown out of the larynx (away) from the nose. The sounds surge into the waggling oral tube that chops them into meaningful sounds. This view permits a more precise account of the true speech apparatus. It is an output instrument that begins at the mouth of the larynx and ends at the outer line of contact of the vermilion border of the lips."

Due to this trade-off, human ancestors with this quirky anatomy were advantaged. They survived to reproduce and leave descendants because they could speak in words. Lloyd DuBrul waxed lyrical about this power: He imagined the synapses in one brain connecting by words with the synapses in one or many other brains, for good or ill. To reinforce his point, we need only think of the power words have to engage the attention of another individual or individuals – for example, the power of a person's name; or the oratorical power of "friends, Romans, countrymen!"; or the galvanising power of the cry "shark!" on a group of swimmers.

Homo Anatomy for Speech

We return to the question: "How well could the Neandertal speak?" There is little fossil record of the soft tissues of the head, so the question needs to be addressed obliquely.

Jeffrey Laitman and his colleagues used fossil skulls and the techniques of comparative anatomy to draw some conclusions on the ability of *Homo* species to speak. The amount of flexion or bending upward in the base of the skull is the fossil clue they used. This flexion has already been mentioned in relation to Lloyd DuBrul's series of primates. Jeffrey Laitman and his colleagues assumed that the position of the larynx in the neck is related to the degree of skull flexion and that that position is important in determining how an animal swallows, breathes and vocalises. They accepted that the dropped larynx makes choking more likely, but noted that the expanded pharyngeal chamber above the vocal folds helps adult humans to modify sounds much more than can infants and non-human animals.

If the flexion of the skull base indicated a dropped larynx (B. Arensburg and colleagues had reservations), then Jeffery Laitman and his colleagues believed that the Australopithecine could not make the range of sounds necessary for speech. Flexion began only with *Homo erectus*, who may thus have been able to make a wider range of sounds than the Australopithecine. Flexion in the Neandertal skull was less pronounced than in the human skull. We shall revisit skull flexion again below.

The other fossil evidence for speech is a hyoid bone found in a 60,000-year-old Neandertal excavated at Kebara in Israel. It was similar to a modern human being's, suggesting that the larynx could have become correctly situated as a "voice box" in them. According to B. Arensburg and colleagues, if the space above the larynx and its positioning were the only criteria required, the Neandertal speech apparatus was probably capable of the range of sounds necessary for speech.

The Wonder of the Speech Process

However, there is a lot more to speech than just the positioning of the larynx. In fact the study of speech is a body of science in itself. Steven Pinker is the main reference for this section.

The process of speech begins with the learnt control of one's breathing, different from the unconscious process of breathing to inhale oxygen and exhale carbon dioxide. To speak, a breath of air is taken in to expand the lungs and is then released in a controlled way. Nariokotome Boy probably was not able to control his rib muscles well enough to do this, because of his narrow vertebral canal. The Heidelbergs and Neandertal probably could control their breathing for speech: The evidence is that their level of social organisation and self-awareness had advanced beyond that of Nariokotome Boy (for example, the improved quality of stone tools, the fashioning of spears, boring holes in bones, grave goods). The process of controlled breathing is a little like the arm of a piper squeezing bag pipes, while the piper tops up the air in the bag of the pipes with frequent puffs of breath. Controlled breathing to speak also conjures up memories of loquacious aunts or uncles (or telemarketers) who apparently can talk nonstop, because they top up the air in their lungs with such quick puffs that one cannot "get a word in edgewise".

The air stored under pressure in the lungs is released through the larynx, including through vocal folds in the glottis, which Greek anatomists named for the mouthpiece of the reed of a flute. These folds can close so tightly that air cannot pass through the trachea at all. But, if the vocal folds are not tightly closed, their opening and closing in the rushing tracheal wind breaks the flow into a series of puffs that we perceive as a buzz, which is called "voicing". This sound can be changed by learnt control of the tension and position of the vocal folds to give the intonations of speech. Voicing is a rich sound ranging from 100 cycles per second in a man and 200 cycles per second in a woman up to beyond 4000 cycles per second. Voicing is the basis of the words we utter.

The voice then passes through a number of chambers comprising the pharynx, the mouth between the tongue and the palate, and then through the opening between the lips, to be appreciated by the receptive synapses in the listeners who Lloyd DuBrul imagined.

An alternative opening is the nose, since we have the ability to lift the soft palate and allow sounds to be modified by the nasal chamber. Lloyd DuBrul described the soft palate as sealing off the airways during speech, but he may not have been completely correct. The fact that the soft palate plays a part in the speech process becomes obvious if you squeeze your nostrils closed while you speak.

Each of these chambers has a length and shape that affects the sounds passing through them, causing the voice to resonate. It is resonance that gives us our vowels. In this respect the tongue is most important since its body can move back and forth, modifying the shape of the chamber. Moving the lips forward also lengthens the chamber. Movements in the root of the tongue change it from being relaxed and flat to being tense and humped. The soft palate can be opened, as mentioned above, adding another chamber for resonance.

The tip of the tongue is a finely controlled barrier to the passage of the voice and is important in forming consonants (which also can be formed by movements of the body of the tongue and the lips). In summary, Steven Pinker wrote that speech actually was created through a combination of gestures made by the tip, body and root of the tongue, the lips, soft palate, nose and the vocal folds. It is amusing to think of Clive Gamble's image of the gesturing honey-bees linked with the behaviour of *Homo erectus* foragers, and also of the gesturing of separately evolved segments of our anatomy: no wonder we "chew over ideas", words "stick in our craw", and we "struggle" to explain some gaffe when we would rather "bite off our tongue". Body language and speech go together.

Steven Pinker did not mention the teeth in relation to speech, he probably took them for granted, but our ability to speak is related to our small bite. Lloyd DuBrul saw the teeth as palisades within the mouth, bounding that potentially unruly organ, the tongue. That is a very useful image. Those of us with false teeth can attest that their absence does result in blurred diction.

Comparing the Neandertal

The evolution of *Homo* species, ever since they became locked into a terrestrial scavenging existence, had been about regaining olfactory prowess to aid survival. There has been frequent comment here on the size and projecting shape of the *Homo erectus, heidelbergensis* and *neanderthalensis* faces and noses. In respect of the Neandertal, commentators have even alluded to their faces as having muzzles or snouts. In marked comparison with us, the Neandertal had huge jaws tightly controlled by powerful muscles, large and well-spaced teeth, and commodious mouths in which their tongues could loll at ease. They had a powerful bite. The Neandertal had a huge nasal cavity and probably a superb sense of smell. We, on the other hand, have a small bite, teeth so crowded that there often is not even space for the wisdom teeth, which therefore often cannot descend. The wisdom teeth are then said to be impacted.

Unlike most animals which bite, our face does not project enough to allow our teeth to be effective offensive weapons. That is really why "man bites dog" makes news headlines. It would actually be hard for a person to bite a dog, unless the dog was gullible and masochistic enough to allow that person a decent attempt.

The reduction in our bite may even be continuing, according to Robert Doolan in *Creation* magazine. He reported how Jack Cuozzo, an orthodontist from New Jersey who studied Neandertal children's fossil jaws and the remains of a group of children who died around 1700 in Connecticut, considered that the relative smallness of modern children's jaws was evidence that evolution can go backwards, or "devolve", which is the reduction in complexity of the human body. Impaction of wisdom teeth is cited as an example of devolution and is said to have occurred because the jaws of children are reducing in size. Devolution of jaws is another curse humankind suffers, due to the fall of Adam.

If the trend to a reducing bite is valid and widespread, as claimed by Jack Cuozzo, a naturalistic explanation would be that our evolution is continuing, assuming there are survival advantages in ever finer speech. A sweet talker is likely to leave more progeny, as we all know.

Our small, dropped, tucked-in face meant that our sense of smell was magnitudes less than it would be in an animal that depended upon it for survival, such as the Neandertal or the dog. The area of our nasal mucosa (the membranes covered in mucous in which olfactory receptors are located) is quite small and the olfactory bulbs in our brain are relatively tiny, almost disappearing under the ballooning, convoluted cerebral cortex (surfaced with grey matter containing thinking modules such as the Broca-Wernicke-Geschwind processors mentioned above).

The Neandertal olfactory bulbs probably were much larger than ours, and linked by networks of nerves to their massive nasal apparatus. Their olfactory bulbs probably accounted for much of the volume of their large brains. (This is certainly the case with the dog, whose olfactory bulbs are relatively huge).

But ... Could They Speak?

To summarise what has been a long discussion, the Neandertal could speak, but not in the very efficient, rapid-fire, clipped or clicked words human beings use as building blocks for the exchange of enormously complex information. Neandertal probably could speak in tongues, but that was not good enough in the end. Writers of fiction have attributed to the Neandertal other means of communication. For example, Jean M. Auel's Clan of the Cave Bear used sign language and John Darnton's remnant Neandertal were of great interest to both the KGB and the CIA for their powers of extrasensory perception. Primates use vocalisation to communicate, but for *Homo sapiens*, in the beginning was the word.

Chapter Eight - Evolution of the Dog Keeper

Along the coastal highway,
Dogs and humans made their way;
Together perfecting speech,
As they strolled along the beach.

Cave Paradise

Caves must have been the refuge of choice for both Neandertal and early human beings. The Neandertal lived in relatively small groups, but did have social cohesion, so may have been able to organise between groups, despite their poor ability to speak in words. The Neandertal must have been formidable foes which evolving human beings had to confront. Caves must have been the places over which the two brainy beings, locked into the process of neoteny and long infant dependency, strove with each other for survival.

In Chapter Six, we considered the origin of the ultra-human Neandertal. In summary, the Neandertal may have entered Europe from the east and spread west as far as Gibraltar, Spain and the British Isles (then connected by the Dogger land bridge). The caves in Spain and Gibraltar became their most western outpost, hundreds of thousands of years later. In the fullness of time, the Neandertal moved east through southern Europe to the Levant, to take up residence there. Their 110,000 to 40,000-year-old remains have been found in caves in Israel, at Kebara (50-60,000 years-old) and Tabun (110,000 years-old); in Lebanon at Amud (50-60,000 years-old); and in Iraq, at Shanidar (46,000 years-old).

I visited northern Iraq briefly in 2005 on behalf of USAID. I was located in the Fertile Crescent at the town of Erbil, which is thought to be the oldest continuously inhabited town in the world. One day, our little group of aid workers was taken for a picnic by our Kurdish hosts. We drove in an armed convoy north up the valley of the Zab al Kabir (the Big River) where the Shanidar cave is located. This cave was excavated by Ralph Solecki from 1953 to 1960. In it he found a number of Neandertal skeletons that showed signs of a tough life – healed fractures. There was one skeleton in particular that may have been deliberately buried, with flowers scattered over the body. The evidence for this was pollen in the grave. This finding gave rise to the image of the Neandertal as the first "Flower People".

As we drove higher towards the mountainous border with Iran, it became clear that Shanidar was just one of many caves in the rocky sides of the valley. The notable thing about the caves was their impressive size, their commanding view of the valley and their accessibility. It was easy to imagine Neandertal families living in them and, later, human beings. Indeed, the Shanidar cave was in daily use by the Kurds and their livestock while Ralph Solecki undertook his dig. The Kurds in the valley, whose dwellings we could see, had been the target of Saddam Hussein's decision to depopulate the Iraqi border and some could have sheltered in the caves.

In the same general area as the Neandertal remains in the Levant, those of modern human beings have also been found, at Skhul and Qafzeh. The remains date to around 100,000 years ago, showing that the two species co-existed in the region for a period of time.

That first time, the human beings apparently did not persist. Christopher Stringer wonders if the human beings could not withstand the cold, or perhaps could not compete against the Neandertal who were already there. The Neandertal and human beings would have competed for the same resources, and so conflict is certainly likely. The fauna of the region included many carnivores that would have been a threat to both the Neandertal and human beings as well. The physically gifted Neandertal may have been able to handle threats from emerging human beings and the carnivores better than our ancestors could.

However, of particular relevance and future importance was that, in the Levant, contact may well have been made between our ancestors and the ancestors of the dog, because it is about this time and in this region that the dog began to speciate from the western Kashmiri wolf, as will be described in some detail later, when I argue that this small wolf began to colonise the caves of our ancestors and adapt to their presence.

Out of Africa for the Third Time

Modern humans arose in Africa. All of those who began the colonisation of the world from about 90,000 years ago, arose from a segment of that African population. Over several tens of thousands of years, these people spread east, along what Spencer Wells called a coastal highway, to south Asia and on to

Australia, or north along a steppe highway to central Eurasia and from there either west to Europe or east to northern Asia and the Americas.

You will recall that the Heidelbergs may have evolved from *Homo erectus* some 500,000 years ago, probably during a period of marked climate change. Christopher Stringer and Robin McKie introduced us to the Heidelbergs in Europe. In Africa the fossil evidence for the Heidelbergs is sparse. Mere fragments of skulls and other parts of the skeleton have been found, but the distribution of the fragments does show that the Heidelbergs were restless people. Until now, we have been able to discuss type skeletons of Australopithecine (Lucy), *Homo erectus* (Nariokotome Boy), the Atapuercans in the Pit of Bones, and the Neandertal as waypoints to our evolution. There is no type skeleton for non-European *Homo heidelbergensis*. Their remains show they were, however, quite active. Evidence of the Heidelbergs has been found at Klasies River, Border Cave, Saldanha, Florisbad and Broken Hill in southern Africa; Jebel Irhoud, Thomas Quarries and Salé in north-west Africa; at Ndutu, Nariokotome, Eliye Springs, Olduvai Gorge, Laetoli, Baringo, Koobi Fora, Middle Awash, Singa and Omo in the Rift Valley and Ethiopia; Zuttiyeh in the Levant; Petralona in Greece; Narmada in India; and Jinniu Shan, Yunxian and Dali in China. The geographical overlay of these locations with fossil finds of *Homo erectus* and Australopithecine suggests the areas had attractions for *Homo* species over very long periods of time. Those attractions may have included caves.

Information from fossils of Heidelbergs may be scarce, but immunologists and molecular biologists can infer the timing and pattern of their evolution. A process of deduction is usually required, using samples from present-day people. A short diversion here will help explain biological techniques.

Fingerprints of Time

The biological analysis of human origins may be said to have begun in the field of immunology, when blood groups in modern humans were compared and waves of immigration within populations were inferred. This was followed in the 1980s by the analysis of mitochondrial DNA. Mitochondria are actually the genomes of ancient bacteria that parasitised other cells. These parasites were co-opted eventually by their hosts to act as their energy processors. Mitochondria are found in the body of the cell, not in its nucleus. Mitochondrial DNA (mtDNA) is therefore in the ovum (egg), but not in the spermatozoa. Thus, mitochondrial DNA traces female ancestors only. Its analysis simplifies the computation of genetic history. Mitochondrial DNA analysis, from 1987, developed as a technique and first indicated the split of human and dog lineages from their common ancestors, each at roughly 130,000 years ago.

Later it became feasible to analyse differences (polymorphisms) in DNA in the nucleus of the cell, where the genome of the individual is actually located. Analysis of nuclear DNA allows richer inferences about the evolution of the donors than does mitochondrial DNA. More recently, analysis of the differences in the DNA of the Y chromosome has become feasible. Genes are parcelled in the nucleus of the human cell in 23 pairs of chromosomes. In males one of these pairs consists of an X and a Y chromosome. In females the pairing is of X chromosomes. Since the Y chromosome is passed only from male ancestors, inferences about a common ancestor are again simplified, as in mitochondrial DNA analysis. In the case of Y chromosomes, however, the inference is directly about the genome of the individual being sampled, not about an ancient parasite of the cell.

Ideally, inferences from DNA analysis are referenced to known fossils, just as the fossils are ideally referenced to the physical environment in which they are found. However, with the Heidelbergs this is not yet possible because of the poor fossil record, a fact that frustrates those searching for detailed clues on the where, when and how of human evolution.

Back to the Heidelbergs

The Heidelbergs in Africa developed advanced technology, as their shafted spears and other stone tools indicate. James Shreeve tells us that, at the town of Katanda on the Semliki River in Zaire, John Yellen and Alison Brooks have unearthed sophisticated bone harpoons and knives that may be over 80,000 years old. Analysis of current human DNA suggests that our ancestors had grown to a population of about 100,000 souls by 200,000 years ago. In appearance they evolved differently to the Neandertal in colder Europe. Their evolution was no doubt still affected not only by competition for resources, but also by changes of climate. Even if these changes were not as extreme as in the higher latitudes, they did affect the savannas, forests and the spread of deserts that constituted the environment of the African Heidelbergs.

The effect of this environmental change on their physical appearance can only be guessed. The fossils at Skhul and Qafzeh do, however, give an idea of the physical appearance of the subset that arose from the Heidelbergs to become human beings. They seem to have been gracile and to have had modern skeletons. The shape of their braincases was also modern overall.

Their faces, however, were unusually short and broad, and they had short, wide noses. Christopher Stringer does not exclaim in surprise about their noses as he did about the Neandertal nose. It appears that the trajectory of their evolution had changed and, in regard to their faces, they had lost their muzzles. Their sense of smell would therefore be less and their bite would be smaller. This trend would have been an exaptation for speech. Neoteny and long infant dependency must still have dictated the desirability of living in caves.

The gracility of the Heidelberg/human skeletons suggested to P. Slurink that cooperation within the group had become more important than individual strength and bulk. Gracility also indicates social changes and increased group size. Richard Alexander argued that cooperation to compete by our ancestors stimulated the evolution of greater braininess, until human beings became their own principal hostile force of nature. The fossil record shows, however, according to P. Slurink, that ecological dominance did not come until late in our prehistory. Then, there is ample evidence of intergroup tension. This tension encouraged within-group cooperation, bigger groups and selective advantage for creativity.

The Heidelberg/humans were becoming much more socially aware – they were evolving the "smarts". The "principal hostile force of nature" that confronted some of the Heidelberg/humans quite possibly included the Neandertal as well as other emerging human beings. We have discussed above how the fossil evidence suggested that emerging human beings could not persist in the Levant, where the Neandertal were "encaved". The Neandertal had powerful physiques, and efficient ears, nose, teeth and eyes. They had a brain most likely tuned for keen observation and olfaction, a fairly simple philosophy of using brawn to settle problems, equivalent facility with tools and weapons as *Homo sapiens*, and a long, impressive *curriculum vitae*, including the ability to withstand cold snaps. If the Heidelberg/humans and the Neandertal co-existed for long periods, the relationship on the "front line" must have been tense, hostile and of evolutionary significance.

The situation was fraught for that subset of Heidelbergs who evolved into *Homo sapiens*. Our mitochondrial DNA has remarkable uniformity, which indicates that, some time about 100,000 years ago, our ancestral population crashed and collapsed through a "bottleneck" down to about 10,000 adult members, in spite of our evolving capacity to speak. The cause of the crash is unknown, but may have been some global catastrophe. In *A Guide to the End of the World*, Bill McGuire suggested that the super-eruption of the volcano Toba in northern Sumatra some 73,500 years ago and the consequent "volcanic winter" that lasted for at least six years may have been the neck of the bottle through which our ancestors had to pass. In an extended winter the Neandertal would have been advantaged by their physiques.

Whatever the cause of stress, our destiny could well have been to become merely interesting fossils upon which Neandertal professors would ponder, some time in the more distant future.

Out of the Bottle

Prehistory shows that our ancestors squeezed through the bottleneck in spite of the much more competent biology of the Neandertal.

The reason for our success, put forward in this book, is that our ancestors were smart enough to have become aware that the small wolves, who had occupied their caves ever since our ancestors' initial thwarted push north into the Levant, were very good sentinels. Our social awareness, our evolved creativity, our cooperating to compete had together exapted us to engage with another species. We were at last becoming a match for the nosey Neandertal because we had become an extended phenotype, as will be discussed below.

And our ancestors told each other about it.

The power of the word is that anyone in the group can benefit from a stroke of genius, luck or wisdom that someone else had, if they are told of it (and choose to listen!), as Steven Pinker noted. Becoming aware of other animals as resources, as servants, has long been recognised as a turning point in the history of human beings. A modern example is the economic historian Walt Rostow who recognised the importance of six legs for the human conquest of the modern world. Walt Rostow wrote the influential book *How It All Began* in which he described societies either "taking off" or crashing.

But the dog is no ordinary domesticated animal. It joined our ancestors as they were on the cusp of becoming *Homo sapiens* and it became a species along with them. We became extended phenotypes. Its presence protected our ancestors and enabled them to survive and further evolve the finely tuned anatomy for speech upon which we have capitalised. This anatomy involved the dropped face, the turned-in hairy nostrils, the crowded tiny bite, the reorganised brain. Our ancestors' survival guaranteed a place in which the ancestors of the dog could adapt and speciate. "It" all began for us because the dog was guarding the runway – while our forebears were in take-off mode. Christopher Wills has an even more dramatic metaphor: Our brains were about to "run away" with us as our brain-culture feedback loop sped into top gear. Our intelligence created ever more complex environments which selected naturally for greater intelligence.

It is likely that the ancestral dog colonised Neandertal caves as well, because there would be vermin and just as many scraps to subsist on as in the subset of Heidelberg/human caves. Why, then, did they not become an extended phenotype of the Neandertal?

The Neandertal was the standard, self-sufficient, conservative "belt and braces" model for human evolution. It had a magnificent physique and sensory perception, was capable of compassion and social organisation. The dogs evolving in their home caves would be of no particular interest to them, unless they were hungry. Their sense of smell was as good as the dogs'. They had no need to share, nor to be aware. They didn't take off because they never thought to fly.

The Race Towards History

Our evolutionary story, after that character-building bottleneck, is one of a race towards history. In the following discussion, Spencer Wells is our main reference. It may be remembered that he leads the worldwide Genographic Project and wrote *The Journey of Man*. The evolving dog was now the constant companion of our evolving ancestors. Together, they formed a very self-aware unit.

The Neandertal also shared our space, until they became extinct some 30,000 years ago.

New technology has allowed the rapid scanning of the DNA of the Y chromosomes for differences between individuals. These differences can be thought of as markers. Scanning these markers allows the genetic diversity in a population to be studied. From the results, common ancestors and genetic waypoints can be inferred and compared with other findings such as fossils and relics, and other mitochondrial and nuclear DNA analyses. To reiterate, the Y chromosome is nuclear DNA, but is passed only from father to son. Like the mother to daughter passage of mitochondrial DNA, this characteristic makes inference simpler when unravelling genealogies of more than a few generations, because otherwise the possible permutations and combinations soon reach astronomical numbers.

Results of Y chromosome analysis and mitochondrial DNA analysis show that in Africa there was great diversity and movement of early human beings. Some human beings had made forays into the Levant, as we already know, but did not establish there, probably because the Neandertal had become a permanent feature. The analysis indicates that only one genetically coherent group left Africa. The common ancestor in that group lived about 60,000 years ago. The group could have left Africa earlier if we assume stable, dominant patriarchies. However, mitochondrial DNA analysis suggests mothers and daughters left Africa about the same time. The departure point from Africa probably was from the north-east corner.

This group of happy dog-keepers (I argue) followed the broad coastal plain, which had been exposed by sea levels fallen some 100 metres lower than today. They travelled around the Indian Ocean to Sri Lanka and the southern tip of India, on to the land mass that became the Indonesian Archipelago and then crossed the sea to the New Guinea/Australia land mass. Clearly they had developed seafaring skills, as one would expect of people who lived along the seashore. Fossils of early human beings at Lake Mungo in New South Wales may be as old as 60,000 years, so the easterly migration must have been quite rapid. The ex-African colonisers were most likely quite comfortable trekking by the sea, as ancient shell middens found along the present coast bear witness. Most of the coastal highway is now under the sea. It will be remembered that *Homo erectus* and the Heidelbergs had preceded them. The coastal migrants do not seem to have turned north to colonise India, but seem to have preferred to travel near the sea.

The human beings who had emerged from Africa later turned north to colonise the Middle East and Levant by about 45,000 years ago, now apparently undeterred by the Neandertal. No doubt their speech had improved and also their organisation of security, especially with dogs on guard. They migrated east and north on to what Spencer Wells calls the steppe highway into central Asia and Mongolia. Others migrated south into inland India or east to South-East Asia and then on to northern China. Those in central Asia migrated west into Europe about 30,000 years ago or east through Siberia and on to the Americas, arriving there only about 10,000 years ago. The Y chromosome of the Africans in the first wave of migrants eventually found its way north about the Pacific and into the Americas as well.

What of those who remained behind in their African caves? Dogs are now as ubiquitous in African towns and villages as anywhere else in the world. The presence of dogs in caves was arguably a critical element in the survival of human beings against the depredations of Neandertal in the Levant. There were no nosey Neandertal in Africa, although there were many other predators. But there were Heidelbergs and there were certainly home caves. The dog, as a fellow traveler, had ample time from its radiation about 130,000 years ago to permeate the home bases of the African Heidelberg/humans. These who were smart enough to recognise the value of the dog as a sentinel would benefit, or would be out-competed by those Heidelberg/humans who had. The process of refining the anatomy of speech could have proceeded within an extended phenotype as already described.

The ancestral speech of the Heidelberg/humans could have been something like the !click language which has nearly four times as many sounds as most modern languages. The !click language is now confined to the San of southern Africa and the Hadza and Sandawe of Tanzania. Perhaps the gradual refining of the anatomy for speech favoured a move to a simpler language, to a more accessible *lingua prehistorica*? The search for that prototype language is another story in itself.

In this chapter I have argued that the dog was a necessary part of our evolution. If the evolution of species is seen as a singular event, the Neandertal appears to be the logical outcome of natural selection within the *Homo* family of species. But the evolution of species is not singular. The singularity of species is a convenient human construct that enables us to discuss the evolution of this or that species. When we begin to discuss the evolution this *and* that species, the matter becomes much more complex. Our ancestors' phenotype extended to include that of the ancestors of the dog. As such, our quite recent ancestors were able to out-compete the Neandertal eventually, as we each proceeded along our parallel paths in life. That self-evident process was a tale of love as well as war, as shown by DNA evidence emerging of hybridisation between Neandertal and human beings, and also the idea of human foundlings being brought up by Neandertal, as told by Jean M. Auel in *Clan of the Cave Bear,* the first of a very popular series of stories about the resourceful young human heroine, Ayla. The saga will not be pursued here because we need to move on to the next chapter, which deals with the evolution of that other component of the extended phenotype, the dog.

Dogs and puppies feature in many contemporary advertisements for material bliss in affluent society. Celebrities and heads of state really must keep dogs if they wish to appear as credible human beings. In India, owning a "doggie" is *entrée* to the wonderful world of refrigerator ownership. In Victorian England the dog was a symbol of "every well-constituted household". In Leo Tolstoy's Russia, a good Borzoi hunting dog was worth three families of serfs. The Romans, Egyptians, Sumerians and so on elevated their dogs to totemic status. At the dawn of civilisation the Natufians appreciated the symbolic value of dogs. Neolithic painters depicted dogs. This chapter has argued that the relationship is even longer: The dog was the necessary component of every well-constituted cave.

The next chapter, Chapter Nine, will explain how our ancestors came to meet the ancestors of the dog. The explanation is firmly naturalistic. In the light of that perspective the explanation can be seen as simple commonsense. Yet the proposition is radical in comparison with many established views on our relationship with the dog. Those views see the relationship as quite short and determined by human priorities. That is, the dog is the product of our own civilisation. It is man-made, a tamed wolf. Those views are common, but they are not sensible.

Some religions have even traditionalised the view that the dog and all other living things are on permanent loan from a deity to human beings. Those views are discussed in Chapter Ten.

Chapter Nine - Dog Meets Man

Cave dwelling may have been tough,
But it was secure enough
For a bit of take and give,
So dogs and people could live.

The zoologist Konrad Lorenz wrote an immensely popular and influential little book called *Man Meets Dog*. It was first published in 1954. Konrad Lorenz founded ethology, which is the study of animal behaviour using zoological techniques. In *Man Meets Dog* he told of a person in the dark tropical night feeling a kinship with the jackals or wolves that waited just out of the range of the human group's firelight. That person tossed them a bone, beginning our relationship with the dog. It was a powerful image of a good intention and an enduring depiction of an appropriate relationship between people and animals.

However, this was not the way that I think the relationship between human beings and dogs began, nor how it evolved. As already mentioned in Chapter Eight, the ancestors of the dog were attracted to *Homo* caves because they offered food and refuge. In this chapter I attempt to see the Heidelberg/human caves from the point of view of the ancestral dogs, that is, naturalistically.

Home, Sweet Home

Many writers visualised original dogs as the unpaid janitors of early human encampments. The dogs scavenged food scraps and human faeces, and eked out an ignoble existence – brutish and short in the extreme – in which they managed to survive long enough to reproduce. The writers' views are quite understandable because this situation can be seen to prevail in squatter settlements around the modern world. I have heard it said – with resigned, wry jocularity – of the dogs in squatter settlements that their muzzles must remain small enough to permit them to lick the inside of an empty food can, or they will not survive to reproduce. Natural selection in a canister! I once saw two dogs in a squatter settlement in Papua New Guinea attack a third with the clear intention of eating it alive – a brutal, indelible scene indeed, and also reflective of the desperate plight of the people in the settlement. In prosperous village situations, dogs, even as scavengers, can do quite well, appearing healthy, well groomed and apparently happy. The dog is an indicator of the human condition.

It may well be that the life of ancestors of the dog was "nasty, brutish and short". There would have been naturally selective pressures for multiple and short breeding cycles, and fecundity. However, the point I would like to make is that the *Homo* home base (caves, at first) was and remains an ecosystem providing the essential biological requirements of refuge and prospect to the animals reproducing within it, including people. Even before the ancestors of dogs colonised the caves, bipedal human ancestors had carried food back to their dependant infants in cave complexes, that were occupied for generation after generation. Those complexes must therefore have provided a feast – well, perhaps not a feast, but enough – of food for other animals capable of living in that environment. Those animals must certainly have included the vermin that infested our ancestors.

Therefore, please consider my suggestion of a food chain, unglamorous although it might appear, that might have nourished other animals in the human home cave. The primary source of energy was food brought home by our scavenging and gathering human ancestors. For the sake of simplicity, the first link in the food chain is proposed to be the skin parasites of our ancestors. Our early ancestors most likely were quite hairy. The smaller front teeth (the incisors) of Neandertal often were worn down like chisels. An explanation offered was that the Neandertal must have used their mouths as tools, to hold fibres as they were twisted into ropes, for example. I have noticed the same sort of wear in the incisors of old dogs and offer a simpler, alternative explanation: Social grooming wore down the front teeth of our hairy ancestors.

Our hairy ancestors must have been bonanzas for skin parasites. One of these parasites probably was the bed bug. Bed bugs must have bedevilled generations of *Homo*. Today, two species of this arthropod are known to have evolved a preference for human blood. Bed bugs are red in colour and flat. They are just visible to the naked eye. They are able to hide in tiny cracks during the day. At night, they emerge to feed on human blood, engorging within about 15 minutes. Female bed bugs lay about 100 to 250 eggs in each batch. The eggs hatch into nymphs, which undergo five moults before maturity. Each stage requires at least one meal of blood before it moults into the next stage.

The saliva of the bed bug is irritating. The torment that our hirsute ancestors must have suffered, is hinted at by an entry in Samuel Pepys' diary for June 1668. On the night of the 11th, he and his wife were made "merry" by bed bugs in an inn in Bath. People in his era tried to fumigate their beds and rooms by burning suffocating concoctions based on animal manure. They tried to outsmart the bugs by placing the legs of their beds in containers filled with water. The bugs, which have no wings, seem to have developed a strategy of dropping on their hosts from the ceiling. Hence this old American verse, courtesy of Philip Street:

The lightning bug has wings of gold;
The gold bug has wings of flame;
The bed bug has no wings at all,
But it gets there just the same.

Bed bugs would have found caves very much to their liking, but there are no records from the *Homo* home caves. But we can guess, from records showing that they adapted well to life in ships. C. S. Forester, the meticulous naval historian and creator of the Horatio Hornblower series, wrote in *Hornblower and the Hotspur* that bed bugs were the worst of the ship-board plagues in the eighteen century, and they were impossible to eradicate. The bed bug must forever have been a given of *Homo* existence. Bed bugs are a favourite food of the cockroach. It therefore seems safe to assume that cockroaches also were a standard feature of *Homo* home caves, because the cockroach has been around for 320 million years. Fossils of cockroaches are among the oldest known fossils of insects.

Cockroach populations can reach huge densities. We can infer that such must have been the case in prehistorical caves, from historical reports. Marshall Laird contributed a paper to a symposium on the spread of pests and disease vectors by commerce, held in Dunedin, New Zealand, in 1983. Because cockroaches were commonplace, he believes they may have been overlooked in the historical record until a particularly heavy infestation was recorded on a Spanish spice ship captured by Sir Francis Drake in the late 1500s. The celebrated historical novelist, Patrick O'Brian, in his unfinished account of the adventures of Jack Aubrey and Stephen Maturin during the Napoleonic Wars, mentions the "voracious cockroaches that no amount of sulphurous fumigation could eliminate from the ultimate depths of the hold, their survivors breeding with extraordinary rapidity." The cockroaches attacked everything edible, including Stephen's carefully collected specimens of animals. This fictional account is probably based on Charles Darwin's experience during his voyage on HMS *Beagle*. In the 1930s, quarantine officials thought it not unusual to kill 20,000 to 50,000 cockroaches in the forecastle of a ship. More than 20,000 cockroaches have been killed in a single stateroom.

Cockroaches would have formed another link in the food chain of the human home cave ecosystem. They in turn would have fed[1] other links in the chain, including rodents such as mice, and birds. Although "mice" is a generic term for small rodents, several species have adapted for living in human habitation. In Iraq, when Ralph Solecki excavated the Neandertal Shanidar cave, he noted that small rodents – a variety of gerbil – had dug tunnels down into the Neandertal remains. Modern-day nomads periodically need to change location and take other measures to control the load of vermin which builds up in their possessions.

Mice of whatever species would have made an

1. Marshall Laird gives an anecdote of a "huge, hairy" spider noisily eating a cockroach in a hotel bathroom, to the consternation of the seated guest.

excellent prey base for predators such as the dog and the cat.

I once volunteered assistance to the Help In Suffering animal and people ashram (sanctuary) in India, in order to research free-ranging urban dogs. The ashram was near Jaipur, in Rajasthan. My visit was facilitated by my friendship with Christine and Jeremy Townend, two Australians who oversaw the ashram. The story of Help In Suffering is told in *Christine's Ark*, which is the biography of Christine Townend written by John Little.

In 1993/4, at the ashram, there was a small staff with families, and a changing population of street or pariah dogs, human "patients", a cat, a monkey, a few cows, camels, horses, and occasional volunteers. The sanctuary ran an ambulance that brought animals in off the street and ran a veterinary clinic manned part-time by municipal veterinarians. Help In Suffering later became involved in an animal birth-control program which, allied with a rabies vaccination program for dogs, markedly reduced the incidence of human rabies in Jaipur.

At the ashram were, among other animals, 20 or more street dogs, two large Doberman pinschers (a male and a female) kept separately, and the cat, which nominally belonged to the manager. The cat was a male tabby, heavier and more muscular than the usual suburban cat. It was about two years old. The cat was gentle and approachable by people, although not effusively affectionate in its behaviour. It was a marvellous physical specimen of its kind. The street dogs, if they could have, would have killed the cat and eaten it. The Doberman pinschers had been boarded at the ashram by a person with whom the management had lost contact. They behaved as though they hated the cat passionately. The cat lived a prudent "arboreal" life, moving skilfully along ledges and so on, just out of reach of all the dogs. In this way it moved about the ashram quite competently. While it tended to ignore the street dogs, it seemed to reciprocate the apparent hatred of the Doberman pinschers and frequently tormented them by posing just out of reach, as they leapt and contorted in their efforts to tear it to shreds. The female Doberman pinscher died. The male continued to go berserk when the cat was near. One day it leapt high enough for the cat to reach down and scratch its nose. The Doberman pinscher died soon after of blood poisoning (septicaemia). The anecdote shows that cats and dogs can cohabit in a relatively "wild" situation. Perhaps ancestral cats were associated, in much the same way as I suggest for dogs, with human home caves from some 130,000 years ago. This is the age Carlos Driscoll and his colleagues estimate, using DNA analysis, for the ancestor of *Felis silvestris lybica* and the "domestic" cat.

Dogs associated with a cave complex would have had indirect access to such animals as birds, bats and unreachable mice by eating the faeces of animals such as the cat. These faeces would have been nutritious, with partially digested animal protein and vegetable matter from the prey's gastrointestinal tract. This may explain the alacrity and apparent glee – the licentious greediness – with which dogs gobble the faeces of cats today, to the shocked dismay of their keepers (who may well themselves enjoy Gorgonzola cheese – bird's-nest soup – black pudding). The caves would also have provided access to human faeces and scraps from meals, to help sustain the dogs.

It must also be said – some images may be distressing – that other food may have included human cadavers and occasional fresh windfalls such as an uncared for infant or a Paleolithic Jezebel. I have a hunch that most burial practices – using graves and crypts, cremation, platforms and niches in cliffs – are attempts to prevent access by dogs to the beloved's cadaver. Evolving dogs would most likely have dragged recognisable parts of cadavers back to the home cave, as is the nature of dogs, causing some shock and horror to the relatives and friends of the deceased, and presumably stimulating an awareness of self in them. Cadavers without any sentimental value probably were given no attention at all, except perhaps to be thrown into a pit as the Atapuercans were or, in historical times, dragged outside the city gates, where dogs, vultures and other scavengers dealt with them in economical fashion.

The most famous cadaver to suffer at the jaws of dogs was that of Jezebel, once Queen of King Ahab of Israel, and power behind the thrones of the two of her sons who succeeded Ahab. The zealot prophet Elijah foretold that Jezebel would be devoured by dogs because she would not recognise Yahweh, at that time a rising expatriate god, as the one true god. And so it came to pass. The upstart army officer Jehu mutinied and then killed or engineered the killing of all the royal family, their staff and their priests, some hundreds of people in total. When he and his cohorts confronted Jezebel, she put on her make-up, appeared at an upstairs window, and bravely taunted Jehu as a murderer of kings. Jehu, at the head of his forces, demanded to know who was for or against him. Two or three of Jezebel's eunuchs, sensitive to the winds of change, threw her out of the window and she was trampled to death under the hooves of the horses below.

Kings 2: 9, 34 completes the story: Satisfied with his work, Jehu went to eat and drink, ordering his minions, "Take care of that cursed woman," he said, "and bury her, for she was a king's daughter". But when they went to bury her, they found nothing but her skull, her feet and her hands. The dogs had devoured the rest of her, as foretold.

Given the short span of time between her death and Jehu's order to bury her body, it seems more likely that the dogs dragged parts of Jezebel off to be eaten in peace, rather than devouring her on the spot. It also seems likely that, had the dogs not been disturbed, her extremities also would have disappeared.

Jezebel's story has been told because of a thought-provoking experience I had at the Help In Suffering ashram. The ashram fronted a road that continued on to cross a small river a couple of hundred metres later. At the back of the ashram was a wadi or gully that ran into the river. An important industry in the town was the dyeing of cotton cloth. The dyes contaminated the river, which therefore ran black. The piece of land that was bordered by the river, the road, the gully and that boundary of the ashram was a place where corpses were cremated. Part of the ashram boundary walls included the wall of a stable with windows that overlooked the cremation ground. One evening, I climbed through a window and walked through the cremation ground, where there was evidence of fires and broken clay pots in which burning buffalo dung (to ignite the pyres) had been carried. Under a sacred peepul tree *(Ficus religiosa)* at a whitewashed shrine, a holy man dressed in white was being tended by two village women in flowing saris. In the quiet of the evening, the setting sun barely visible as an orange ball through the smoke of cooking fires, the black river forming one border, and with the tall tree and graceful figures of the people, the scene was surreal and spiritual. A procession of mourners arrived, bearing a simple stretcher on which was a body so tiny that it barely was visible within the sling of the stretcher. It was the body of a woman known in the ashram, who had died of typhoid. The procession carried wood for her pyre. This wood is brought in to the area by camel trains from faraway dwindling forests.

The next morning, as I waited with the few other human inmates outside the kitchen for our vegetarian breakfasts, I saw one of the ashram pariah dogs with a sacrum in its mouth. The sacrum is the fused lowest part of the vertebral column and in people includes the remnants of the tailbone. The sacrum that appeared at breakfast most likely was from the just cremated body. As is the nature of dogs, this dog had brought its trophy back to the ashram, where it lived. Confirmation of the sacrum as human could not be made because the dog, noticing the interest with which I regarded its prize, slunk away with its booty. The implications of the experience shook me. How would a country of more than a billion people dispose of its dead in the future, given a widespread tradition of cremation on pyres? Years later I wrote a poem to sort out my thoughts on my visit to India. One verse is relevant here:

Camel trains carry pyre wood.
The rich burn as well as they should,
But the poor tend to be underdone –
Not enough wood for everyone.

But, cadavers aside, as a food of last resort for the dogs there would always have been those cockroaches replete with bed bugs …

Thus the Heidelberg/human cave could have been sufficient to the radiating southern wolf as a place of food and refuge. The evolving ancestral dog would have been subjected by its new home to developmental constraints, which probably included remaining small, watchful, opportunistic, fecund, not too savage and having cosmopolitan tastes in food – and it barked. In this way it benefited evolving humans smart enough to be aware of it as a sentinel. Its phenotype was being extended to them for their survival – and the dog's. Incidentally, one way the human genotype would have extended to the dog in beneficial behaviour is grooming. It is usual to see people in many varied walks of life pick through a dog's fur for fleas (and ticks, where I live), or to pat, bathe or comb it, or, very recently, to apply spot-on anti-parasitic treatments to it. In return, for many of us, the feel of the dog's coat is pleasant and it seems likely this is an evolved benefit for us.

However, one of the main benefits to the dog, like Richard Dawkins' beaver and its dam, is that the *Homo* cave, with its food chain, would have afforded protection from the many carnivores of the day, which would eat the dog and compete with it for food. Why did the ancestor of the dog not find *Homo* caves before 130,000 odd years ago, when its DNA indicated it speciated? One can only guess. Perhaps the caves were not organised sufficiently; perhaps the Neandertal had not yet arrived from western Europe; perhaps *Homo heidelbergensis* had not yet emerged from Africa. Earlier *Homo* would have eaten the dog's ancestors, without a second thought.

This chapter has shown that the *Homo* cave would be a habitat suitable for an animal, such as a small southern wolf, to exploit and adapt to; those adaptations would be exaptations for its evolution as an extended phenotype with *Homo sapiens*.

Next, in Chapter Ten, I explain why I consider that the ancestor of the dog was a small southern wolf, probably the animal called the western Kashmiri Wolf, that was in the area when the African *Homo heidelbergensis* emerged on their first foray out of Africa. The ancestors of the dog adapted to this event in ways that are explained in Chapter Ten also. Mainstream mindsets that tend to begrudge the dog its status as a species will also be discussed in Chapter Ten.

Chapter Ten - Caveo Specus Canis!

(Beware of the cave dog!)

When we think laterally,
Dogs arose naturally:
Variation over time,
Within Darwin's paradigm.

On a few occasions, people who learn that I am interested in the origin of dogs have said seriously, "'Dog' is 'God' spelt backwards, you know". This is one of those statements that stick in one's mind like nonsense rhymes. Is the statement inane or does it have substance?

This book develops the argument that dogs and human beings have co-evolved as extended phenotypes. That is, figuratively speaking, they are mirror images of each other, and complementary in fact. "Dog" is (almost) a mirror image of "God". So, perhaps you will excuse a very short pause on the *Homo* beaten path for me to pose the question – what is God?

Many religions teach that God is Love.

Canadian philosopher John Leslie applies this statement in a practical way: "God" names the principle that ethical requirements are creatively powerful. I find that his interpretation fits well with a naturalistic perspective, because the connection of ethics with the productivity of a group, its culture, can be seen as a survival trait. To see God as a principle, implies making choices within a complex social environment. Making such choices would hardly be practicable, without words to share information and allow discussion within a group. A group of animals that could enunciate well, would think better collectively and survive, where less gifted groups might not. In the context of the argument put forward in this book, our survival by enunciating words was made possible through our interactions with the dog. An ethical human society would consider dogs with respect; that is, would regard them as subjects, not objects (It would be easy to digress further, and argue that our footprint of ethical requirements naturally would extend to the other animals upon which we depend).

As individuals, many of us do identify with the dog in a subjective way. Even the poorest of the poor in slums will rise up against dog catchers, if they are considered cruel. In Moscow dogs have been allowed to adapt to the subways. They alight at stations as they choose. We extend to dogs our sense of fair play. Community anger is intense when dogs are mistreated although we turn blind eyes on the mass abuse of food animals. Many of us confer quasi-human status on dogs. As Stephen Clark points out in *The Moral Status of Animals*, for many of us the dog is an honorary human being.

However, for others of us, dogs are dirty, shameless slaves fit only for food or fur. They are objects.

Collectively, we objectify the dog because it is convenient to do so and because, in the West at least, the dog's separateness is ordained by religion and by statute: It is merely one of the domestic animals that we are entitled to use.

The following discussion is about refocusing our collective view of the dog, such that our ethical stance can be broadened. In a refocused, broader view, "dog" may indeed be another way of spelling "God".

The Domestication Red Herring

The perception of animals as somehow domesticated for our use is possible because of our concept that human beings are separate from animals – and even from nature. This is an untenable premise because we are an animal (not to put too fine a point on it, try running with your hands in your pockets), but the attitude is so prevalent that it is necessary to devote some time to it now. To presume an animal is the product of domestication is to steal from it some of its natural status; in this context, some of its doginess.

Early human beings and other *Homo* may have identified with other animals genuinely. In many cases, hunter-gatherers and nomads, for example, still do. Some present-day cultures may still use systems of totems and taboos to recognise the relationship between people and other animals. But, for the purpose of this book, I think it correct to say that dominant world religions assign to human beings privileged alignment with God. Human beings are the centre of the universe because it is to us alone that certain truths have been revealed through scriptures or books, or through the teachings and behaviour of individuals who, through a process of self-realisation, have achieved transcendental understanding. The result is the orthodox certainty that the world was created for our enjoyment. Even modern science sees something godly about tinkering with animals for human benefit, and restates the orthodox attitude as a kind of religion.

Of formal religions, one example is the Biblical model in which God gave dominion over animals to Adam and, later, to Noah and his sons: God's gift countenanced the use of animals by human beings even unto the plate – or down to the Vet's for neutering or to the pound for euthanasia. Since human beings learned how to create certain animals – with or without God's blessing – the animals became, in a sense, man-made. They are called domesticated. The process of domestication involved the taming of those animals, bringing them into the human fold, controlling their breeding and exploiting them for human purposes. Once made, domesticated animals are the property of their makers. In this limited view, their usefulness to us over-shadows an appreciation of their fundamental being, whether they are pets or have commercial value. We can under-appreciate their biology (and ours) because their status is derived from their making.

A more naturalistic explanation of domestication was suggested by Francis Galton writing in 1865. In his model, animals most likely were domesticated in a haphazard process, successful only with those wild animals that were hardy, had an inborn liking for people, loved comfort, were useful, bred freely, and were easy to look after. Francis Galton was a great naturalist and explorer, a cousin of and an enthusiastic supporter of Charles Darwin. While Francis Galton grants target animals some determining effect in the domestication equation – they were suitable for domestication or not – he sees the equation operating anthropocentrically. He foresaw that those animals that were not tractable were "doomed to be gradually destroyed off the face of the earth as useless consumers of cultivated produce".

This gloomy prediction carries much weight – economically useful species are now bred in their billions, at the expense of many species threatened by the "civilisation" of the natural environment. However, many other species have adapted to the civilised environment and have thrived, without being domesticated in any meaningful sense, proving that adaptation to human presence is a naturally selectable trait. Francis Galton did allow that some prehistoric genius may have hit upon the idea of domesticating animals to exploit them, thus the process perhaps was not haphazard. He argued that this brilliant idea might then have been taken up by other early human groups.

Francis Galton realised that being "domesticatable" was a survival strategy for some species. Yet the word is not found in dictionaries or spelling checkers. Jared Diamond used the word "domesticable" in *Guns, Germs and Steel*, his short history of everybody for the past 13,000 years. However, he seemed to use it only as grammatical licence and did not delve into its evolutionary significance. Jared Diamond placed the dog in with other domesticatable animals, as an instrument of modern human development.

As to the timing of domestication, the orthodox view is that the domestication of animals occurred in the later stages of human evolution, at the point of civilisation, because a high level of technique was thought to be required of early humans. Within this view, the domesticated dog occurred about 12,000 years ago with the first signs of human civilisation. Writers often cited the first confirmed domestic dog find as being a five-month-old dog found buried with an elderly human under a Natufian dwelling in Israel. The Natufian is the earliest known human civilisation. The elderly person's hand had been arranged to lie along the dog, indicating affection and, hence, domestication. Locating domestication of the dog by archeological reference received tacit support in 2009 from the way mitochondrial DNA data were analysed by Jun-Feng Pang and a large team of collaborators. The team argued that the dog was derived from taming of wolves 16,500 or fewer years ago, south of the Yangtze River. They suggested it was bred to be eaten.

Tying the origin of the dog to first archeological evidence of human civilisation prevents wider-ranging discussion. In effect, this limited discussion tends to ignore the vast bulk of the human story, given the evidence of tool making over hundreds of thousands of years, cave paintings, human migrations and so on, not to mention reports of the dog in the Belgian Goyet cave 31,700 years ago and the French Chauvet cave 26,000 years ago, to be discussed in the next section. It also ignores human seafarers at least 60,000 years ago and the deliberate movement of cuscus possums for food between islands in Melanesia as long ago as 20,000 years, and the likelihood that forests and probably other plant species were manipulated by people to make them more attractive for prey species well before 12,000 years ago.

Many writers on dogs assume the dog was originally useful to evolving human beings for hunting game. An argument supporting this assumption was the parallel sociality of human hunters and wolves. Roberta Hall and Henry Sharp explored this topic in *Wolf and Man: evolution in parallel*. They compiled a series of papers illustrating the similarities between wolf and human evolution. Among the contributors was Michael Fox who described the parallels between wolf packs and human tribes in the practise of rituals, use of tools (he saw the wolf's teeth as tools), control of conflict, dominance hierarchies, xenophobia, food sharing and cooperative hunting.

The wolf pack was popular as a model for human evolution, when a pugnacious attitude to nature was more common. An example was that of Carveth Read, who published *The Origin of Man* in 1925. Among the characteristics of human behaviour he noted, was a social organization "like that of wolves". Carveth Read differentiated the hunting pack (a hierarchy searching for food) from a herd (organised defensively). The hunting pack psychology included thrill of the chase; passion of the kill; variable gregariousness; lack of sympathy for and aggression towards all those outside the pack; territoriality; leadership and loyalty; subjugation to the needs of the pack; a hierarchy; and capacity for strategy. Robert Ardrey, a popular writer in the 1960-70s on human evolution, developed this idea into *The Hunting Hypothesis*, with human beings cast as pack predators, to the dismay of humanist writers.

In a recent paper, "Co-evolution of humans and canids", Wolfgang Schleidt and Michael Shalter have taken the argument to an extreme by speculating that human ancestors teamed up with herd-following wolves, adopted their lifestyles and, through a process of mutual cooperation, co-evolved.

The hunting hypothesis is, in my view, unsatisfactory. Not all wolves hunt in packs, their relationship with people was competitive rather than complementary, and their social economies were different to those of human groups. In his contribution to *Wolf and Man*, Henry Sharp compared how the indigenous Chipewyans, in far northern America, and the wolf packs, organised to exploit the caribou. Whereas the wolf used a strategy of overkill to spread caribou carcasses widely as food stores which are accessible during the denning season, the Chipewyans established home bases at which the meat could be dried and preserved for times of scarcity. Where the wolves depended upon their physical prowess to detect, cut out, pursue and pull down their prey, the Chipewyans used ambush techniques and weapons.

The evolving dog was not an integral part of the evolution of *Homo sapiens* because it was a hunting aid or hunting colleague. *Homo* species had, for millions of years, thrived without it. The evolving dog was an integral part of human evolution because we became extended phenotypes.

A Naturalistic Perspective on the Origin of the Dog

The naturalistic perspective on the origin of the dog is that the ancestral dog speciated in Heidelberg/human home caves from some 130,000 years ago, and thus dogs and people co-evolved as extended phenotypes. That is the thrust of this book. It is no surprise then that a dog skull discovered in the 1860s in the Goyet cave in Belgium has recently been found to be 31,700 years old, using very sophisticated dating techniques. The report originated from the work of a team of researchers at the Royal Belgian Institute of Natural Sciences, led by Mietje Germonpré. The teeth of the skull were larger than in the dogs of the present. The skull had a wider cranium and shorter muzzle than a wolf skull and the dog must have been as large as a shepherd type. DNA analysis of a number of skulls from Belgium, Ukraine and Russia uncovered substantial genetic diversity, suggesting that the wolf populations of the time were quite large. The team found that the Goyet dog was clearly different to wolves, both fossil and recent. In the same report on the finding in the

Goyet cave, there was mention of footprints in the Chauvet cave in France. The footprints were 26,000 years old and belonged to a child and a dog. They wandered along quite comfortably together – there was no suggestion of a chase – and the two could have been companions.

These finds are strong support for the argument that the dog was a partner in our evolution, rather than a relatively recent man-made object. They have been challenged recently by the archeological team of Hannes Napierala and Hans-Peter Uerpmann (reported by Bruce Bower, 23 July 2010), who claim that their investigation of a 14,000-year-old dog jaw fragment, found in 1873 among human remains in the Swiss Kesserloch cave near the German border, is the earliest reliable evidence of domestication of the dog. Mietje Germonpré reportedly debates this statement, and I agree that there is ample evidence to the contrary, as will be discussed shortly.

Strangely enough, the naturalistic perspective, which is a biological model, actually confirms that the dog is Man's Best Friend (or, at least, our oldest colleague) which is an anthropomorphic model, but without anthropocentric assumptions of ownership and objectivity. The relationship need not have been intimate or friendly, yet would still reflect enduring interdependency.

Here is another anecdote from the Help In Suffering ashram. It is about Grumpy. Grumpy was a male dog who lived in association with a shop, where the shopkeepers fed him vegetable scraps. Grumpy's relationship with his human associates is probably the most common form of the human/dog relationship in the world today. It was a natural relationship – Grumpy's keepers did not own Grumpy as a pet.

Grumpy was so named by a young Scottish

volunteer because he snapped at all ashram staff – even at her, whose intensely compassionate nature usually soothed animals. He had extremely bowed fore-legs, due perhaps to nutritional deficiencies or the heritable disease chondrodysplasia. He was an ill-natured, unprepossessing dog – quite difficult to like. He had good reason be irritable: a cart had run over his paw. The skin was scraped off and the bones exposed. The wound was slow to heal, partly because Grumpy was so difficult to handle that dressings could not be changed easily. Grumpy remained at the ashram for several weeks.

During that time, Grumpy's associates, the shopkeepers, visited him regularly, bringing him tomatoes to eat, since Grumpy was particularly fond of this fruit. At no time during their visits to the ashram did Grumpy's associates show other signs of liking him, although they spent time sitting near him, talking to each other. The relationship appeared to be one of being in an association, rather than one of possession. There was no obvious reason for them to be concerned about Grumpy, since street dogs were plentiful and one could easily have been encouraged to replace him as a watchdog. In time, Grumpy was returned to the environs of the shop and I assume he re-established his residence there.

The idea of two species being companions for one another suggests an evolved association and gives a glimpse of the beginning of such relationships. Such an explanation is more satisfactory than the limited dimensions imposed by the concepts of domestication and pet ownership. The story of Grumpy shows that a broader theoretical base than human self-interest is necessary when considering the animals with whom we now associate.

When the ancestors of dogs first moved into

Heidelberg/human caves there would at first have been no relationship between the two species, other than that of two animals sharing an ecological niche. With the passage of time, each species adapted to the presence of the other. In the case of the dog, it adapted to the natural environment of the human home cave, which included the presence of evolving human beings. The caves presented natural opportunities for any animal that could adapt through a process of natural selection to fit better in that environment and thrive as a species. The dog can be seen as an outstanding opportunist who thrived naturally. The emerging human being can also be seen as a natural opportunist, but one who, by adapting to the presence of the dog in the human home cave by learning its body language, could evolve in such a way that it would, in a relatively short time, speak words and so out-compete the Neandertal. While the Neandertal and the human being trod the earth together, the direst competition would be over caves which were critical to the survival of each. This is the story I have developed in this and other sections.

Taking the Dog out of Dogma

To repeat, the relationship between people and dogs is natural and co-evolved. They are two animals that adapted to each other and to their common ecological niche, which initially was the cave. They became interdependent. So far as I am aware, no-one else has argued that the dog and people are extended phenotypes, but there are several authors who have used a naturalistic perspective to write on the evolution of the dog. For them the explanation of the dog as a product of human ingenuity is not satisfactory. This is my view also, and I have to admit to considerable impatience with those who look no further back than evidence of "civilisation" for the beginning of the dog/human story, even though we have a history of cave-dwelling magnitudes longer. Following is a brief review of some writers who influenced my thinking, even though some of them do also have the short view of the dog/human relationship. For the sake of brevity, only those who wrote post-1990 are discussed.

Helmut Hemmer used a broad variety of methods to develop his statement on the origin of the dog. He compared the wolf, coyote, jackal and dog using the paleontological record, social behaviour such as vocalisation, and biological features such as their anatomy and serum protein patterns. On this basis, Helmut Hemmer concluded that a primitive form of wolf was widely distributed over disparate and separate areas from Europe through Asia to North and Central America. In that wide area, evolution of the wolf ancestor proceeded at different rates and in different ways, those to the north adapting to Ice Age conditions and becoming the northern grey wolf – most often recognised as the "wolf" in popular Western literature. In the Arabian Peninsula and South Asia, however, the more primitive southern wolf form persisted in relative evolutionary isolation. It is this form that most resembles the primitive dogs such as the dingo, the Madagascar primitive dog, the Basenji, Samui and South-East Asian pariah dog. Immunological studies provided particular support for the argument of an early branching of the dog from the evolutionary path of the grey wolf.

It is a matter of conjecture as to when the branching of the dog from the primitive southern wolf may have occurred. Helmut Hemmer noted the relatively small size of carnassial teeth in the southern wolf. Carnassial teeth are the last premolar in the upper jaw and the first molar in the lower jaw in dogs. These teeth are in apposition and act as shears for cutting meat. The smaller carnassials suggested an early branching of the southern wolf from the evolutionary path of the northern and central wolves in which much more powerful carnassials evolved. It may be that this branching occurred in an even more restricted zone than that occupied by the southern wolves, perhaps involving only *Canis lupus pallipes* and *C. lupus arabs* in India and western Arabia. These animals have large, round eyes, have short, sharp barks, and hunt singly, in pairs or in small groups. They may be scavengers rather than pack hunters of large game. These features differentiate them from northern wolves and their behaviour more closely resembles that of the dog. Helmut Hemmer's analysis tended to place the speciating southern wolves/dogs in the area where the Neandertal and Heidelbergs confronted each other – and at about the same time.

There is limited archeological evidence for this: Kolska Horwitz thought that partially digested bones – usually in caves – at Israeli archeological sites from the Kebaran period onwards (some 60,000 years ago) in fossilised scats possibly were left by dogs, but noted that many other carnivores were in the area.

Mitochondrial DNA analysis was a tool to which Helmut Hemmer did not have access, but Carles Vilà and his colleagues did. They reported the analysis of sequences of mitochondrial DNA in samples collected from 162 wolves and 140 domestic dogs (representing 67 breeds of dog). Samples from five coyotes and 12 jackals were also analysed, although the results for these were not reported in detail. The researchers considered that the results showed that the ancestor of the dog is the wolf, not the coyote or the jackal, because there is much greater divergence of the dog sequences from coyotes or jackals, and less divergence from those of wolves. The relationships between the wolves and the dogs were categorised statistically.

The results suggested that there was sufficient difference between the wolf samples and most of the dog samples to show that divergence of dogs from wolves occurred much longer ago than the longest time allowed for agriculturists to domesticate dogs. Because divergence of wolf mitochondrial DNA sequences from the coyote's was about 0.075 (or 7.5 per cent) and the divergence could be dated from the fossil record at one million years ago, and because the divergence of most of the dog mitochondrial DNA sequences from the wolves in the survey was 0.01 (or about one-seventh of the mitochondrial DNA sequence divergence of wolves from coyotes), Carles Vilà et al suggested that the divergence of dogs from wolves could have occurred 135,000 years ago. The situation was complicated, they wrote, by the possibility of subsequent interbreeding between dogs and wolves. Carles Vilà et al acknowledged that the results were estimates, but pointed out that they showed that the split of the dog from the wolf was much more ancient than about 14,000 years ago. They hypothesised that early dogs may not have looked very different to the wolf, until human beings became sedentary.

Helmut Hemmer's "primitive southern wolf" may itself be something of a can of worms. A clade describes those animals that share a common ancestor. Dinesh Kumar Sharma and his colleagues reported mitochondrial DNA analysis of dog and wolf samples that indicated that the Indian region was the likely cradle of wolf evolution, but the wolves were actually of three clades or lineages. Two of these clades, the peninsula Indian wolf and the Himalayan wolf, which extends from eastern Kashmir to eastern

Nepal, did not contribute to the origin of the dog. The third lineage was the wolf-dog clade and is of course the one that interests us. Only the third wolf, from western Kashmir, was in the wolf-dog clade. This clade may have been in existence for two million years according to fossil evidence. Within the wolf-dog clade, dogs appeared to split from wolves about 150,000 years ago. On this basis, Helmut Hemmer's ancestor of the dog, the primitive southern wolf, may be the western Kashmiri wolf.

Susan Crockford is an archeozoologist who is particularly interested in how a domestic animal is generated from a wild ancestor. She considered that the traditional definition of domestication was no more than a myth – "domestication dogma". She found no evidence in the archeological record for the deliberate domestication of the dog by people. She considered that mitochondrial DNA analysis failed to show an association between regional subspecies of wolf and particular types of dog. Rather, it seemed to her that any subspecies of wolf could have generated the dogs of today. Susan Crockford saw founding populations of one or more species of wolf colonising human habitations in a process of proto-domestication and speciation. The founding population consisted of animals that were tolerant of stresses caused by the proximity of human beings. The proto-domestication process could be rapid because it did not depend upon mutations arising in the animals' genotypes. Once the animals had survived proto-domestication they proceeded to be classically domesticated by people using conscious artificial selection.

Susan Crockford considered that any captive or commensal (living together or, in context, sharing our table) population of animals could be domesticated through this two-step process. Her hypothesis was that proto-domestication was controlled by the rhythmic release of thyroid hormone, not directly by the genes of the animal. Although thyroid hormone was ultimately controlled by genes, the rhythm by which it was released was species specific. Thus, she would see the dog as a variant of wolf with a different rhythm of thyroid hormone, which unstressed it enough to begin living in proximity to the dreaded human being. Since thyroid hormone controlled growth rates in organ systems, the rhythm of its release, which was heritable and sensitive to selection pressure in an as yet unknown way, resulted in a suite of physiological changes. In the generation of the dog from a type of wolf, these changes included age at sexual maturity, size, coat colour and behaviour. Susan Crockford believed the process of proto-domestication of some animals occurred about 14,000 years ago, and that the change from the wild to domestic form took much less than 100 years. Susan Crockford has begun a life quest to prove her hypothesis on the rhythmic release of thyroid hormone.

Ray and Lorna Coppinger are biologists who do not think that wolves were domesticated by people to be hunting companions. They believed that the dog was a product of natural selection as a consequence of the ecological niche made by human organisation in middle-Stone Age villages. They saw the dog as adapted for scavenging human waste found in continuously occupied settlements. Therefore, they argued, the dog could not have evolved before 12-15,000 years ago, when such settlements came into being. Like Susan Crockford, they saw the process of adaptation occurring rapidly, in fewer than 100 years, due to high selection pressures in the new ecological niche. The Coppingers commented on the phenomenal plasticity of the dog phenotype, in spite of there being no discernible difference in the genotypes of the various breeds. The development of the wolf was constrained by the need to survive in its natural environment, and its phenotype was consequently much more conservative than the kept dog.

Ádám Miklósi seemed to estimate appearance of the dog at about 10,000 years ago, but noted that even if the event occurred earlier, 100,000 to 150,000 years ago, in evolutionary time it had happened very quickly, compared to symbiotic relationships between other species, for example, cleaner fish and their clients.

Lesley Rogers and Gisela Kaplan are quite open-minded about the hypotheses on the domestication of the dog and, in *Spirit of the Wild Dog*, agreed that dogs and human beings must have altered each other's lives. They doubted that morphological changes caused by domestication of the dog occurred only as recently as 12,000 to 14,000 years ago.

Janice Koler-Matznick revisited the origin of the dog in an impressively succinct, technical review in *Anthrozoös*, the journal for human-animal relations. She compared the behaviour, morphology, fossils and genotypes of dogs and grey wolves, and mentioned the problem of hybridisation between dogs and wolves. The grey wolf was the one of legend and is called *Canis lupus*, other wolves tending to be assigned subspecific names such as *Canis lupus pallipes*, the Indian wolf. Janice Koler-Matznick pointed to the long-term hierarchical pack structure of the grey wolf, which was different to that of the dog. She thought grey wolves were more likely to attack and eat human beings, especially children, than associate with them, and was quite unconvinced that the grey wolf would drift into human habitations and specialise on human waste. She regretted the dogmatic approach to naming the various wolves that has significantly skewed the way the origin of the dog is studied. For example, she thought the ancestry of the pariah dog had not been investigated in any depth because it had been assumed to have descended from the grey wolf. Much more likely candidates for the ancestor of the pariah were, for her, the small Indian wolf or the ancient *Canis lupus variabilis*, whose fossils were found in Choukoudian (also spelt Zhoudoukian) in China, associated with *Homo* artifacts. This site is 50km from Beijing.

Janice Koler-Matznick accepted mitochondrial DNA analysis as a useful tool, provided one was aware of its limitations and of the assumptions upon which the conclusions were based. She seemed comfortable with a time of separation of the dog at 76,000 to 135,000 years ago from a wolf line, but considered that dogs may have been descended from a now extinct canid that was related to the wolf. She commented on the complication that, for their whole period of existence, there was the possibility of hybridisation between the various types of wolves. However, she made the point that, even though hybridisation may have occurred, dogs and wild wolves did not normally socialise together. The small Indian wolf, for example, and Indian pariah dogs were not known to hybridise even though they were similar in many respects, and the wild Indian wolf populations were now small and fragmented. Janice Koler-Matznick concluded that the dog most probably descended from a medium-sized generalist canid, which might now be called *Canis familiaris*, and which occupied the pariah niche commensally until some members became domesticated.

On the matter of hybridisation, it may be of interest

that Aristotle[1] (384-322 BC) referred to the then contemporary practice of tying up female dogs so that wolves might mate with them, noting that many were devoured "if the wild animal does not happen to be excited for mating". At the turn of the 20th century, Jack London referred in *White Fang* to a similar practice whereby Alaskans tied female dogs out to be mated with wolves, and Farley Mowat also refers to this practice in *Never Cry Wolf*, as told to him by Ootek.

Hybridisation also can be seen within the global dog populations. The data of Adam Boyko and his many colleagues, who have analysed the mitochondrial DNA of a large number of dogs in several countries, show that the dog spread rapidly after original domestication – which they estimated at 15-40,000 years ago – and reached high, effective population sizes. It was a winner, its genes flowing between continents. This success complicated the analysis of DNA to determine the origin of dogs, however, because dog genes also flowed back and forth as dogs accompanied human colonisers. In some areas (central Namibia, Puerto Rico) indigenous genes had been swamped by dogs brought in by colonisers. In other areas, non-indigenous dog genes may have been quickly removed from village dog populations. Adam Boyko et al showed that the interpretation of mitochondrial DNA results was still far from exact.

Some authorities who accept mtDNA evidence for the longevity of the relationship have adjusted their view of the relationship. They consider the dog as separate from other domesticated animals; as the first animal to be domesticated. In his keynote address

1. In his history of animals Aristotle credits self-awareness and a sense of fair play to wolves: "... around the Matois lake too they say the wolves are habituated to the men who bring in the catch of fishes, and when they do not give them a share they destroy their nets as they are drying on the ground."

to the Centre for Human Biology at the University of Western Australia, Colin Groves, an authority on clades, accepted that the dog is a quasi-species in a symbiotic relationship with human beings. He hypothesised that the relationship intensified in the Holocene (that is, from say 12,000 years ago) such that each animal – the dog and the human being – domesticated each other, as Jonica Newby had suggested in *The Pact for Survival*. Respectfully, I beg to differ on this point. Human beings could not have been domesticated by the dog because our ancestors had not been in anything other than a "domestic" situation for more than a million years. Similarly, my argument is that it was in a natural process, longer than 100,000 years, that the dog became a species within *Homo* caves; there was no human purpose involved until late in this process. The Composite Conversationalist Hypothesis goes further than symbiosis. From the vantage of the present we can see that the extended phenotype, hand-in-paw, ambled into a certain future, naturally.

After consulting the writers above, and many others, and considering the power of the theory of origin of species by means of natural selection, it seems to me that a reasonable and economical explanation for the origin of the dog is as follows.

The ancestor of the dog was the western Kashmiri wolf, one of three Indian wolf species living in the area that the Heidelberg/human beings entered when they emerged from eastern Africa. The Kashmiri wolf radiated into *Homo* home caves (perhaps possibly including those of the Neandertal, where no interdependency occurred). In the caves the two species adapted to the presence of each other and the dog quite likely evolved through a process of proto-domestication, as hypothesised by Susan Crockford. However, unlike her proposition, proto-domestication proceeded over a long period, as noted by Carles Vilá and his colleagues, and Lesley Rogers and Gisela Kaplan, and the Kashmiri wolf became the dog. During this period the evolving dog was subject to constraints to its survival but, on balance, adapted naturally in its ecosystem and thrived. It became a permanent feature in the caves, moving with our ancestors on their migrations, acting as sentinels and changing their environment such that *Homo* variants with better capacity for speech could evolve into human beings and, in the fullness of time, move north into the lands of milk and honey, in spite of the Neandertal.

The next chapter deals with the dog as it adapted and evolved as an extended phenotype of the human being.

Chapter Eleven — Faithful Fido

Toby's at home with humankind,
To hunt his food would be a bind;
In return for being on guard,
He simply seeks your kind regard.

In the previous chapter, domestication as dogma was discussed and the argument advanced further that evolving people and dogs adapted to each other's presence. This chapter is chiefly about the adaptations that led to the dog. Charles Darwin used the success of breeders of animals as a model for discussing natural selection, but he noted that the effects of artificial selection are minimal in comparison with natural selection – although we may manipulate animals at great expense in the present, natural selection determines their future.

Man-made Animals

Human beings can "create" a version of a domesticated animal in a highly artificial situation. Silver foxes with dog-like docility have been "created" in an experiment in central Siberia, which has continued for more than 40-years. These foxes are valued for their furred skins and are farmed as an alternative to trapping, but are very susceptible to stress when enclosed, to the point where their productivity falls. The experiment aimed to breed docile foxes that would produce furs more efficiently. The research was originally led by Dmitri Belyaev. He was succeeded by Liudmilla Trut. The experiment was not a success from a fur farmer's point of view, in that the changes that happened in the foxes led to unacceptable piebald fur patterns. However, the experiment did give insights into the process of domestication.

Foxes were selected by introducing a gloved hand into their cages. Those that attacked the hand immediately or showed exaggerated fear were excluded from the breeding program. In a few generations, selecting even just this one phenotype created a line of foxes that were docile, particularly those bred from a female called Laska. Their coat colour changed to piebald in the process.

The results corroborate some matters raised by the Coppingers and Susan Crockford (mentioned in the previous chapter). These were the speed with which change in the foxes occurred, the cascade of effects that flowed from selecting for only one phenotypic criterion in the foxes, the probable effects of hormones on the phenotypical outcome, and the effect of the founder, the famous female Laska. The changes appear to be the consequence of selecting for stress tolerance, as hypothesised by Susan Crockford in relation to proto-domestication.

But the experiment showed that exceptions do prove the rule: Naturally selective logic prevails. Although Liudmilla Trut and her colleagues have given us a glimpse of a process that could have produced the cave dog in theory, in practice they manipulated the foxes in a highly artificial environment. In the wild, foxes that lacked fear of human beings would soon end up as their apparel, even if they were piebald. The same development constraint would face the evolving ancestors of the dog in caves. It is therefore highly unlikely that the evolving dog made a giant leap in only 100 years or so to become a dog. It seems far more likely that the dog ancestor retained its wild phenotype and its fear of *Homo* (especially hulking ones who conversed in tongues) for a much longer period, as it evolved in the caves into a species. This is in line with the comments of Carles Vilà and colleagues reported in Chapter Ten. A fearful dog is a much better sentinel than a phlegmatic dog, and is a more effective partner in an extended phenotype than a docile dog.

The Dog as Dog

Writers on the subject of dog domestication express no doubts that the domestic relationship between human beings and dogs had an effect on the morphology, the appearance, of dogs in general. As you will realise, I would prefer to use a term "adapted to human presence" or some such, rather than "domestication", but the discussion would become unwieldy. For this chapter I am forced to dismount from my high horse and use directly the terms "domestic" and "domestication".

Anatomical changes are an established way of differentiating domestic dogs from the wolves. Frederick Zeuner provided an early guide to the differences:

- domestic dogs differ from the wolf type in having barrel chests and thus having out-turned elbows so that there is a difference between the widths of their front and back gaits;

- they have a shorter and straighter back;
- they carry their tails upright;
- they may have lop-ears in the adult;
- their eyes are round and directed forward;
- their faces are shorter and broader and have a pronounced "stop" where the forehead rises from the bridge of the nose; and
- their teeth are smaller, especially the canines and carnassial (shearing) teeth.

This is a rough guide only. Modern zoo-archeologists use very sophisticated techniques. The skull in the Goyet cave in Belgium, mentioned in the previous chapter, was subjected to detailed measurements, which showed it differed from both fossil and recent wolves, and was from a dog. These measurements included the lengths of the carnassials (shearing teeth) and tooth row, and the widths of the snout and the braincase. The results are then indexed to allow for differences in body size and then analysed for statistical significance.

The anatomy of an animal is not the only thing affected in the process of domestication. Helmut Hemmer argued that, compared with their wild ancestors, domestic animals in general had a reduced appreciation of their environment, expressed as:

- attenuated behaviour;
- weaker flight and alarm reactions;

- less overall activity and sensitivity to environmental cycles;
- looser social bonds, reduced complexity and differentiation in society, and often an increase in social compatibility; and
- intensified sexual activity and perhaps intensified intra-specific aggressiveness.

Helmut Hemmer noted that there was a relationship between coat colour and domestication, which we saw in the Russian silver foxes. In dogs, for instance, he suggested it was conceivable that the initial breeders of the northern wolf to the dog (his proposition, not mine) began by eliminating the genetic alternative of the wolf's grey coat. His rationale was that there is a relationship between melanins that produce coat colour and the biochemistry of environmental appreciation. In simpler terms, from his point of view, it can be seen to be in the interests of the dog and its domesticator that its coat colour be clearly different from the wild type. On the other hand, as we know from our discussion of Susan Crockford's hypothesis and Liudmilla Trut's experiment with the silver foxes, if the evolving dogs adapted to human presence by becoming stress-tolerant, friendlier animals, similar phenotypic changes would have occurred naturally. Very savage animals were unlikely to survive in an intensely social environment such as a cave containing armed *Homo*.

The dog's phenotype probably changed in intangible ways as it adapted to the human beings evolving in its cave. These would have included an exquisite understanding of human body language, as Jonathan Bradshaw says in *The Secret Life of the*

Dog. You can test for this sensitivity in your dog by reaching for the lead. The sensitivity accounts for the usefulness of the dog in detecting seizures in people, among other things.

Complementary sleep patterns have been shown to exist and it seems fair to argue they evolved. Graham Adams has shown that the sleeping pattern of suburban dogs is different to that of their human keepers, the dog sleeping in 16-minute cycles of sleep followed by wakefulness for five minutes, while their keepers slept for several hours in cycles of deeper sleep of about 90 minutes duration. Graham Adams noted that sleep in a group of dogs was asynchronous, and considered this would give a pack of dogs an adaptive advantage for survival. He found that, while the short sleep cycles and asynchrony led to barking that disturbed neighbours, those who kept dogs for protection as well as companionship welcomed their dogs' watchfulness. In another study, Graham Adams and K.G. Johnson found that barking of other dogs was the main stimulus for barking by study dogs, and it is intriguing to imagine the signalling effect between allied caves and home bases tens of thousands of years ago.

The changes in the dog's phenotype were reflected in reciprocal changes in our phenotype, as already expounded. The dog did not do all the adapting.

There is no doubt that our association with dogs changed the phenotype of the dog in basic ways, well before the advent of breed societies and "designer" dogs fewer than 200 years ago. The finding of the 31,700-year-old dog skull at the Goyet cave in Belgium shows that dogs have their own evolutionary history that is paired with our own. If the dog barks like a dog; behaves like a dog; smells and feels like a dog; and looks like a dog, why call it a subspecies of wolf? Why not call it *Canis familiaris,* as once was commonplace? The fact that the dog can, in highly contrived and rather fraught situations, breed with the wolf is hardly the point.

Original Din – the Watchdog

In *The Wealth and Poverty of Nations*, David Landes argued that the politically based division of the world into East and West power blocs is now less relevant. With the globalisation of trade, a more appropriate division based on wealth and history may now be "the West and the Rest". This division fits the discussion in this section very well. "The West" can be defined as societies having governments that are well structured and can afford to control dog populations. As such, those populations do not approximate a natural situation.

In "the Rest", the dog is represented by the ubiquitous pariah dog and a sprinkling of the "doggies" of the expanding middle class.

The pariah quite probably is the most numerous type of dog in the world. In this book, the pariah dog is considered to be the archetypal dog in early human settlements.

Epstein defined the pariah dog: "The term pariah is derived from the Tamil 'pariayan'; literally meaning 'drummer', it is applied to members of a low caste in southern India. As applied to domestic dogs, it denotes a group whose individual members are generally distinguished from the majority of other domestic dogs in that they are not attached to human masters, frequently not even to certain households; they are not bred, reared or protected by man, but eke out a miserable existence scavenging on whatever they can pick up in the streets and outskirts of towns and villages."

In many village situations, I hasten to add, the dogs do not have a miserable existence, and a small proportion will be "owned" in the sense that they are collared or tagged in some way.

A fairly common, but I think erroneous, view of the pariah dogs is that they somehow are degenerated domestic dogs which, although having become semi-wild, retain the habit of associating with human beings. Perhaps this view arises because some settlements of "the Rest" provide temporary residence for expatriate workers who may abandon dogs that they had befriended when they return home. The dogs may form packs and survive long enough for one or two to be befriended by some other person.

The reality is that the pariah dog has always been there, at least since we existed. I concur with Brian Vesey-Fitzgerald's comment, in *The Book of the Dog* published in 1948, that "we are not conditioned to expect in a wild or semi-wild animal the characters and qualities of the domestic dog, and, when we find them there, we leap to the conclusion, without the least justification, that the domestic dog must originally have been responsible for them".

Brian Vesey-Fitzgerald argued that "the great difference between the Pariah and the wolf or the jackal is that, while both wolf and jackal can be tamed (and even, on occasions, trained), their young are born wild and continue to be born wild even after generations of breeding between tamed adults, whereas the Pariah cannot only be tamed and trained (even, on occasions, as adults), but the young, after only two or three generations, are born tame. Furthermore, the Menzels, from the depth of their great experience, believe that it would be possible to breed out of Pariah dogs, and in a comparatively short time – every known type of domestic dog".

The Menzels to whom he referred, Rudolph Menzel and Rudolphina Menzel, were keen observers of the pariah dog. They argued that pariah dogs constitute a well-defined group of natural variants of the dog and that the pariah genotype should be preserved.

It is not difficult to imagine that, within caves, and increasingly over time as human beings became less dependent on caves, subniches would exist for variants of the evolving dog. The Menzels considered that the pariah could be classified into five types of natural variants:

- Type I — Heavy extreme type (Sheepdog-like)
- Type II — Heavy medium type (Dingo-like)
- Type III — Light medium type (Collie-like)
- Type IV — Light extreme type (Greyhound-like)
- Type V — Small-grown type (Toy-dog-like).

It is interesting that, more than 50 years after the Menzels' studies, Paula Wapnish and Brian Hesse found the Menzels' classification to be of enduring practical value, when they investigated the historic dog burials at Ashkelon on the southern coastal plain of Israel. At Ashkelon, well over a thousand puppies and dogs were found to have been deliberately and individually buried some 2500 years ago, for purposes unknown. At first Paula Wapnish and Brian Hesse tried to categorise the skeletons according to published assumptions on the use of ancient dogs, for example, as bred for hunting, but finally concluded that the Ashkelon dogs could best be described as similar to "ancient Near Eastern and modern dogs of no particular ancestry". They found the Menzels' typology to be the best way to describe the Ashkelon dogs, that is, as pariah dogs naturally adapted to the regional climatic conditions. I also feel comfortable thinking of the pariah dog as "The Dog", unalloyed by deliberate human intervention.

The characteristic of the pariah dog that the Menzels identified as being of prime importance to human beings was: "He is a born *watchdog*. Because of his distrust and sharpness he is incorruptible; because of his high reactivity he can sense the approach of strangers even at a great distance, and not only can he warn of the approach of human beings, but also of alien animals, *i.e.* jackals and cats."

The veterinarian Michael Fox drew on the research of the Menzels when he studied pariah dogs in south-west India. Michael Fox considered that pariah dogs could be classified into three types on another set of criteria: Type 1, which are home owned and tend not to roam far from home; Type 2, which are home owned but free ranging; and Type 3, which are ownerless and free ranging. Michael Fox also considered the pariah as perhaps the dog prototype of those living with "early agricultural man in village communities". He noticed that, if a focal food source exists, such as a butcher's stall, there is a tendency for even Type 3 dogs to develop a territorial situation similar to the other types. If any Type 3 dogs are provided with a home by a person, a similar "sociofugal territoriality" is introduced that disrupts pack structures.

H.G. Wood used the Biblical record to determine that pariah dogs infested Jewish towns in Palestine in the time of Christ. The dogs were scavengers that had to be "cleared off periodically with poison". This is a fair description of current policy on street dogs in countries of "the Rest". Although the clearing off process may employ more modern poisons, it is often protested by human beings living in the area who identify with the dogs. H.G. Wood also noted that pariah dogs were easily made into pets.

The capacity to entice human protection, then and now, can be recognized as having survival value for the dog. The more desirable its characteristics from a human point of view, the greater the chance of its survival and multiplication. In David Paterson's film *The Secret Life of the Dog,* Jonica Newby refers to the "cuteness factor" in relation to the way puppies can capture the hearts of human beings. The Coppingers point out that the physics of birthing and feeding from a nipple mean that young dog and wolf pups must look alike at first, the cuteness wearing off if the wolf pup does not imprint on human beings within a few days. In adult dogs, the ability of the dog to "meet the market" can be seen as a trait subject to natural selection. This can explain the enduring variability of form which characterises modern breeds of dogs.

Chapter Ten and this chapter argue that the dog is the current end result of an animal that adapted within an ecological niche that contained evolving *Homo sapiens*, as well as several other animals. The niche consisted of subniches, particularly when *Homo sapiens* moved out of caves. The dog was not the purposely created product of human ingenuity. Even when people had learnt to control the breeding of the dog, end results were ephemeral, although no doubt very satisfying for their breeders. Charles Darwin noted that British breeds of pointers, hounds and greyhounds that were exported to India "degenerated" in appearance into the pariah type of dog, even though no cross-breeding occurred with the pariah. He noted that even bulldogs were susceptible to this effect, their muzzles becoming finer and their bodyweight less. Spaniels apparently were more resistant.

Breeds of dog may be seen as being inherently unstable and requiring the constant intervention of dog breeders. This is particularly obvious since the advent in less than 200 years of a plethora of dog breeds. Some of these dogs now can only be bred artificially, that is, by insemination or caesarian delivery. They could not be selected naturally. The others would, if left to their own devices, soon become approximations of the pariah dog, as Charles Darwin noted. The vast bulk of dogs in "the West", however, are neutered and transparent to natural selection, although of great social and economic importance. A naturalistic perspective shows that these dogs are supported by quite small populations of parents who provide replacement puppies.

According to Jeb Brugmann in *Welcome to the Urban Revolution*, half the world is now a city. Some 3.5 billion people live in cities and soon there will be 5.5 billion city dwellers. The Menzels' concern 60 years ago that the pariah genotype should be preserved may prove to be prescient. It is this watchdog genotype that is the real part of our extended phenotype, not the breeds of dog. The dog is very adaptable. But if planners trying to manage the monsters that cities have become do not include a naturalistic perspective in their choices of policy, then a part of our extended phenotype may become extinct. We depend upon the phenomenal sensory powers of the dog in more, not fewer, ways. We depend upon its adaptability more, for companionship and health benefits. These economic and social benefits are well documented in a wide range of books on dogs and their sensory abilities.

The Neandertal was on a trajectory of braininess and nosiness and brawn for 400,000 years. In comparison, our trajectory as an extended phenotype has just begun, with a focus on braininess and communication by words, leaving the watchfulness and smelling to the dog, and leaving the evolution of the refined anatomy for speech to us. A naturalistic perspective warns us not to cut off our nose to spite our face.

How good is the dog's sense of smell in comparison with ours? In one word: phenomenal! The capacity varies between people and between dogs, some are better than others and the skills can be refined through training. Among the many authors who provide comparisons, Steven Lindsay's *Handbook of Applied Dog Behavior and Training* is comprehensive and gives some astounding examples. Butyric acid is a component of human sweat and so is an important signal to the watchdog. According to Steven Lindsay, a dog can *in theory* smell one gram of butyric acid in an envelope of air the area of a large city and 100 metres high. That is, detect human sweat one million to one hundred million times better than can a person. The membranes covering the convoluted nasal turbinate bones in a dog's muzzle would, if stretched out, extend from 20 to up to 400 square centimetres and carry 250 million receptors. Human nasal membranes cover merely 2 to 4 square centimetres and carry five million receptors. These membranes capture molecules in the air on mucous-coated microscopic hairs called cilia. Cilia are actually extensions of the receptor neurons leading to the olfactory bulbs situated quite nearby in the brain. As already mentioned, these bulbs are much larger in the dog than in people.

Human beings can detect a thousand different smells; dogs probably can detect more. At least a thousand types of olfactory receptors are known to exist. The dog is better able to identify odorants with large numbers of carbon atoms in the molecule.

Practically, the dog is a phenomenal detective: It is thought that it can differentiate the rate at which scents arrive at each nostril and so deduce the direction of a trail because it can also detect deterioration of a scent with time. A trained dog can smell a human fingerprint on a glass slide up to six weeks old indoors, or two weeks old outdoors, and not at all if the slide is underwater. A dog will avoid the odour of a psychotic child and it may be that the trained dog's ability to detect seizure and hypoglycemic patients may be due to differences in their smells, not just due to changes in body language. It is for this reason that dogs have a role in preventative medicine (detecting cancers in the doctor's waiting room has received media coverage recently) and in monitoring environmental contaminants. In Queensland, the State in which I live, dogs are now used with success to detect colonies of Fire Ants, the important foreign invasive pest. There is a difference between breeds of dog when it comes to detecting smells, but this does not seem to matter in relation to hearing. A dog can detect higher frequencies of sound than can people, and is better at identifying direction of sound because of its movable ear blades.

The sense of smell is an ancient sensory ability. Up to 1 per cent of the mammalian genome is involved in the detection of odours. That is a large proportion of a mammal's genes, when one thinks of the huge workload of the genome. Clearly the anatomy of smell is of practical importance as well, as this determines the volume of sensory input. Steven Lindsay warns against over-generalising from data, but it does seem safe to assume that the dog's world view is different to ours because of its ability to detect and assess smells.

Our dog Toby is now old and, dare I say it, often

behaves like an elderly human as he puzzles over sounds that he has just missed. He often makes mistakes in visualising objects. But his sense of smell still appears good. If he is late for his morning walk with our neighbour, Margaret, and she has left, I have seen him hunt about on her trail and then run off in the correct direction. In the interests of perfect truthfulness, however, I must also add that Margaret often waits for him, knowing that his hearing is no longer perfect enough to detect her footfall early and arouse me from sleep, to let him out.

On the matter of people/dog world views, for us the person we are talking to is *over there*. For a dog the visual evidence of a person must seem like the mere centre of gravity of a whole wafting body of smell. One thing that puzzles me is, if Toby's sense of smell is so good, why does he sniff urine scent (for example) so closely and for so long, and have to be dragged away by his lead? Just how interesting can the "message" *be*?

The power of smell and the "texture" of odours are difficult to convey in print, but Patrick Süskind manages to do so very well in his rather confronting novel, *Perfume*, which is the story of a serial killer who invents an irresistible perfume made of maidens' sweat. In his novel, he uses his powerful talents for description to show that human olfaction can be acute, and that smells can be almost tangible in their richness. His skill gives the reader some inkling of how surreal must be the dog's sense of smell.

Toby's sense of smell ensures that he remains important to us as our watchdog, even though he is failing in many other ways as he approaches 98 in dog years. That's pretty old. He is lying odourously on the carpet now and snoring gently. I look at his cauliflower ears and his grey muzzle and brow, and think of the days when he was a force to be reckoned with on the beach, digging like the mad terrier that is part of his constitution, and how he once was an enthusiastic sailor-dog, perhaps due to that part of him that was the dingo that accompanied human seafarers to Australia. Or perhaps, I think, is it the German Shepherd in him that allows him in his dotage to relax confidently into our care? Or should I be using the Menzels' typology: Types V, II and I? It doesn't really matter. Toby and we are an extended phenotype – the Composite Conversationalist.

Chapter Twelve - Closing Words from the Composite Conversationalist

'Though we may be an integral part
Of the sweep of Darwinian art,
We are neither artist nor model;
Only paint — not even the easel!

Together we have travelled over continents and through millions of years in time. Charles Darwin's theory of the origin of species by means of natural selection enabled us to discuss the origin of people and dogs, and me to hypothesise the Composite Conversationalist. The two species co-evolved as an extended phenotype that continues to evolve. In the brain of that extended phenotype, the cerebral hemispheres can be seen as being in people and the olfactory bulbs as being in dogs. That is a dramatic image, but it is only one twist of the kaleidoscope. The complete picture is of two animals cooperating to survive in spite of the superb Neandertal and despite a variety of finely tuned wolves. These two animals literally had their backs to the wall of their cave, but together they managed to finesse their way into the future.

Because of the evolved interdependencies or complementarities, the two animals seem very useful to each other. The dog, for example, is useful to people primarily as a watchdog, but also for food, clothing, leather, medical and scientific research, guarding, hunting, warmth, fighting, tracking, drug detection, searching for people, controlling rodents, recreation, display, racing, companionship, social status, a cult object, a seeing/hearing aid, detecting seizures and other medical/psychological conditions, facilitating interactions by adults and children, a model for evolution, military/police sentinels, bomb detection, messengers, environmental hazard detection, invasive pest detection, a pawn in sexual politics and on and on. People can be seen as useful to the dog for organisation, food chain, protection, leadership, grooming, companionship, shelter, healthcare in affluent societies, and preservation of the dog as a species.

In this book many topics were discussed. On the time scale of evolution, the Pleistocene was a relatively short period, but one of turmoil: Climate changes and tectonic upheavals alternately lured and punished species, and drove them back and forward between latitudes. Arboreal species ancestral to human beings were in Africa. Some five to six million years ago their trees were shaken so severely that they eventually became terrestrial and bipedal. On the ground they faced predators that must have terrified them out of their not so tiny minds, but they survived by adapting to life in caves. There, by chance, they survived by a "strategy" of increasing nosiness, braininess, dexterity and social cohesion. The natural processes that made this strategy viable were their omnivorous diet, neoteny and language. In the caves, infants were protected through years of dependency. The

Homo species learnt to make tools and weapons, and began to exploit and increase their territory by expeditions from family caves. The expeditions became migrations out of and about Africa, but cave dwelling for families remained an imperative for survival because of dangerous predators and other bands of *Homo.* At any one time there may have been different but similar *Homo* species in the same area. For the sake of concentrating on the argument for the Composite Conversationalist, I referred to only a few type species for which there is good fossil evidence. I offered them as waypoints for human evolution.

The Neandertal evolved 400,000 to 500,000 years ago at some place, perhaps north of the rising Himalaya mountain chain. They perhaps entered Europe from the east, displacing the existing *Homo* species. They moved west until they reached the Iberian Peninsula, then moved south-east into the Mediterranean, eventually spreading to the Levant where they took up residence in caves. It was here that the Neandertal first met our ancestors. The meeting was not initially propitious for our ancestors, who were repulsed, but contact with the ancestors of the dog had been made and our ancestors became aware of them. From then on, the dog infested the caves of our ancestors, alerting them to danger and allowing *Homo* variants with the anatomy for speech to survive and evolve in the caves. The dog adapted to cave dwelling with our ancestors and evolved into a species. An extended phenotype was born, the Composite Conversationalist.

The Composite Conversationalist managed to displace the Neandertal from the land of milk and honey and move north to occupy Eurasia. David had finally prevailed against Goliath. The Neandertal became extinct some 30,000 years ago.

I think the key quality the dog brought to the

extended phenotype was a phenomenal sense of smell. By learning to depend upon the dog's sense of smell, flatter-faced variants of our ancestors could survive and thrive, because they enunciated words better. For this reason I went into some detail in quoting experts on the evolution of speech and the dropping of the face in the evolving human being. My aim also was to show that survival of the evolving human being was not obviously logical. Logically, the end product of the human evolutionary process was the Neandertal, not the human being. Logically the human being could not have evolved unless it was in an extended phenotype. What the human being brought to the extended phenotype was ever-improving organisation, which was a haven for the evolving dog so long as it could adapt to our rather quirky behaviour, even now, of treating it as both an object and a subject. Eating it and loving it. Dog evolution too does not immediately appear logical. The superb wild wolves appear to be the logical end products of natural selection. The dog in comparison became attenuated. But its evolutionary trump cards were its watchdog abilities and tolerance of people. Human organisation did the rest, providing it with protection as well as a conveniently located food chain.

The Composite Conversationalist Hypothesis sees the dog actually in the caves (which may have been large complexes) evolving adaptations to an existence very different to the wild wolves, some of which were roaming in packs large enough to pull down large game. I have described the *Homo* cave as an ecological niche, in which the primary source of energy was food brought in by evolving human beings. Other animals adapted to the niche as well. We were all animals under one roof. The juxtaposition of the caves, evolving dogs and evolving human beings occurred fairly recently (say 130,000 years ago) and in a specific area (say the Middle East). I think this is a naturalistic perspective that is more realistic than the merely comforting view that the dog wanted to be liked by us.

So far as I know, wherever there are people there are dogs. It is easy to think now that the dog is our friend because the dog it knows best is probably you. The dog we know tends to be neutered, dependent, a little confused and maybe a bit phobic, overweight and, in the social sense, dog-challenged. In most of "the Rest" of the world, dog and human societies operate in parallel, but interdependently. There, it is a dog eat dog world. In that world, the imperative for the dog is: "get myself a piece of human organisation and defend it, hopefully not to the death." For people the imperative is: "get myself a dog and hopefully it will defend my little piece of organisation to the death." This is a naturalistic perspective. Two animals need each other. The dog is not just a privilege or an object to be regulated by a bureaucracy.

There are problems in the relationship. They need to be managed because the relationship is important and enduring. There is a developing literature, especially in sociology and psychology, which substantiates that comment. The International Society for Anthrozoos (ISAZ) has been an important contributor in that regard. It was established in 1991. The Society publishes research and other papers in *Anthrozoös*, its journal, and conducts annual conferences. Urban animal management is taken seriously in some communities. In Australia, the Institute of Urban Animal Management was established about a decade ago. Enlightened city designers do take our animal natures into account. They design for refuge and prospect, and include dog-keeping among human activities. The dog provides security and assists us to conceptualise space, which helps us to live harmoniously in ever-denser situations (see John Calhoun). These situations, for complex reasons, depress our rate of reproduction naturally. A rare few enlightened urban planners do take the dog into consideration when designing parks and public areas. Urban solutions become ever more important as populations of cities balloon.

A naturalistic perspective can be an informative alternative to the usual way of seeing other animals, which tends to have human economic self-interest at its core. But, the reason the dog appears to offer so many economic benefits to people is that its qualities complement deficiencies in our nature. We may be more dependent than we realise upon the other animals we exploit without a care. We are animals who are adapting to a diet based on intensively farmed animals and plants, for example. Issues for us are lactose intolerance, triglycerides, chemicals and antibiotic-resistant bacteria, herbicides in crops, ethical costs of cheap animal protein, etc, etc. "New" diseases emerge as we push into the habitats of other animals. The naturalistic perspective is a way of discussing these issues.

The dogma of domestication has been discussed. The dogma is either that the dog was given to us by God, to do with as we choose, or that we ingeniously created the dog from the wild wolf, to do with as we choose. These alternatives are indulgent red herrings that distract us: We are an animal like all other animals. The Composite Conversationalist continues to evolve. The dog continues to be a part of our phenotype. We cannot ignore this for the sake of convenience.

In Charles Darwin's time, "no greater act of the human intellect, no greater gesture of humility on the part of man has been or will be made in the long history of science" than admitting that we are animals (Loren Eiseley). Since then, it has become a cornerstone of biology that we *are* an animal interacting with many animals in the natural world.

I think it is OK to talk to your dog. I talk to Toby all the time. I do not talk to Toby about the meaning of life. He would not be interested, having abrogated the cerebral side of things to his human partner in the extended phenotype. Our conversation is a one-sided kind of small talk, and my words have a definite grooming effect on him. The words exercise daily the bond between us. Toby communicates by body language and trusts implicitly that I will respond. This trust places quite a burden of responsibility on me for his welfare, but this is only to be expected: we are a Composite Conversationalist; we share each other's phenotypes.

Epilogue

The television news
Puts me in other persons' shoes;
I feel their fear and pain
As Earth breathes out, then in again.

There but for God's good grace,
Or for Chance's uneven pace,
In their place would I be,
Bereft and out of harmony.

Burned, surged, shaken,
Blown, bullied, irradiation;
Whatever the trouble,
Dogs help us search through the rubble.

References

Following is a list that is indicative of books and papers I have consulted over the past 15 years, to speculate on the co-evolution of ourselves and dogs. I think it was necessary to prospect in a wide range of sources to consider the subject. After all, to think about the dog is also to think about the human condition, as I hope this book shows. Mattei Dogan and Robert Pahre put my case elegantly in *Creative Marginality: innovation at the intersections of social sciences*.

The power of Internet search engines to research topics is awesome and addictive, but these engines cannot access many of the older references. These need to be found in central libraries and second-hand book shops. The search can be worthwhile because, often, naturalist writers from a bygone era had a thoughtful appreciation of nature. I offer an analogy in explanation: An expert tracker following the spoor of a wounded buffalo must find the buffalo eventually, but it pays for him or her to stop and look around every so often, just in case the buffalo has turned around. This is the situation imagined by G.K. Chesterton, the celebrated English writer and poet, in his poem *The Song of Quoodle*: "And Quoodle here discloses ... The Noselessness of Man." Quoodle was, I think, a dog who would have detected the presence of a tiger stalking his keeper, who thought he was stalking the tiger.

Strangely, though his was a naturalistic perspective, Chesterton's deep religious beliefs prevented him from accepting the origin of species by means of natural selection.

Abercrombe M., Hickman C.J. and Johnson M.L., 1987. *The Penguin Dictionary of Biology*, Penguin Books, London.

Adams, Graham J., 1993. 'Sleep-wake cycles and other night-time behaviours of the domestic dog *Canis familiaris', Applied Animal Behaviour Science*, 36:233–48.

Adams, Graham J. and Johnson, K.G. 1994. 'Behavioural response to barking and other auditory stimuli during night-time sleeping and waking in the domestic dog *(Canis familiaris)', Applied Animal Behaviour Science*, 39:151–62.

Aiello, Leslie C., 1994. 'Variable but singular', *Nature*, 368:399–400.

Aiello, Leslie C. and Dunbar, R.I.M., 1993. 'Neocortex size, group size, and the evolution of language', *Current Anthropology*, 34(2):184–93.

Alexander, Richard D., 1990. *How did humans evolve? Reflections on a uniquely unique species*, Special Publication No. 1, Museum of Zoology, University of Michigan, Ann Arbor.

Ardrey, Robert, 1977. *The Hunting Hypothesis*, Fontana Books, William Collins Sons, Great Britain.

Arensburg, B.; Schepartz, L.A.; Tillier, A.M.; Vandermeersch, B. and Rak, Y., 1990. 'A reappraisal of the anatomical basis for speech in Middle Paleolithic hominids', *American Journal of Physical Anthropology*, 83:137–46.

Aristotle, see Balme; Thompson.

Arsuaga Ferreras, Juan Luis, 2002. *The Neanderthal's Necklace: in search of the first thinkers*, (trans. Andy Klatt), Four Walls Eight Windows, NY.

Auel, Jean M., 1981. *The Clan of the Cave Bear* (first in the Earth Children series), Coronet Books, Hodder and Staughton, Great Britain.

Balme, D.M. (ed. and trans.), 1991. *Aristotle: history of animals*, Books VII–X, Harvard University Press, Cambridge.

Bar-Yosef, Ofer, 1994. 'The contributions of Southwest Asia to the study of the origin of modern humans', in Matthew H. Nitecki and Doris V. Nitecki (eds), *Origins of Anatomically Modern Humans*, Plenum Press, New York:23–60.

Beck, A.M., 1979. 'The ecology of the urban dog', in Robert D. Allen and William H. Westbrook (eds), *The Handbook of Animal Welfare*, Garland STMP, New York:51–5.

Beck, Alan and Katcher, Aaron, 1983. *Between People and Pets: the importance of animal companionship*, Putnam Publishing Group, New York.

Beck, Leslie J. and Watson, Richard A., 1987. 'Cartesianism', in *The New Encyclopaedia Britannica*, Goetz P.W. (ed.), vol. 15, Britannica, Chicago.

Becker, R.F., King, J.E. and Markee, J.E., 1962. 'Studies in olfactory discrimination in dogs: II. Discriminatory behavior in a free environment', *Journal of Comparative and Physiological Psychology*, 55(5):773–80.

Bekoff, Marc, 2000. *Strolling with our Kin*, American Anti-Vivisection Society, Lantern Books, Booklight Inc., NY.

——, 2000. 'Paxton's panorama: naturalizing the bonds between people and dogs', *Anthrozoös*, 13(1):11–12.

Beilby, Walter, 1897. *The Dog in Australasia*, George Robertson and Company, Melbourne.

Benton, Ted, 1993. *Natural Relations: ecology, animal rights and social justice*, Verso, London.

Blumler, Mark and Byrne, Roger, 1991. 'The ecological genetics of domestication and the origins of agriculture', *Current Anthropology*, February, 32(1):23–54.

Boesch, Christophe, 1990. 'First hunters of the forest', *New Scientist*, 126:20–3.

Bökönyi, Sandor, 1989. 'Definitions of animal domestication', in Juliet Clutton–Brock (ed.), *The Walking Larder: patterns of domestication, pastoralism, and predation*, Unwin Hyam, London:22–7.

Bonner, John Tyler, 1980. *The Evolution of Culture in Animals*, Princeton University Press, Princeton.

Boule, Marcellin, 1923. *Fossil Men: elements of human paleontology* , transl. Jesse Elliot Ritchie and James Ritchie, Oliver and Boyd, London

Bowcock, A.M.; Ruiz-Linares, A.; Tomfohrde, J.; Minch, E.; Kidd, J.R. and Cavalli-Sforza, L.L., 1994. 'High resolution of human evolutionary trees with polymorphic microsatellites', *Nature*, 368:455–7.

Bowdler, Sandra, 1981. In 'Comments', concerning Brian Hayden's paper 'Research and development in the Stone Age: technological transitions among hunter-gatherers', *Current Anthropology*, 22(5):519–48.

Bower, Bruce, 2010. 'World's oldest dog debated', *Discovery News*, 23 July, http://news.discovery.com/animals/oldest-dog-fossil.html

Boyko, Adam R.; Boyko, Ryan H.; Boyko, Conn M.; Parker, Heidi G.; Castelhano, Marta; Corey, Liz; Degenhardt, Jeremiah D.; Auton, Adam; Hedimbi, Marius; Kityo, Robert; Ostrander, Elaine A.; Schoenebeck, Jeffrey; Todhunter, Rory J.; Jones, Paul; and Bustamante, Carlos D., 2009. 'Complex population structure in African village dogs and its implications for inferring dog domestication history,' *Proceedings of the National Academy of Sciences, Early Edition*, www.pnas.org/cgi/doi/10.1073/pnas.0902129106.

Boyle, Katherine V., 1990. *Upper Paleolithic Faunas from South-West France*, BAR International Series 577, Oxford.

Bradley, O. Charnock, 1959. *Topographical Anatomy of the Dog*, Oliver and Boyd, London.

Brain, Charles Kimberlin, 1981. *The Hunters or the Hunted? An introduction to African cave taphonomy*, University of Chicago Press, Chicago and London.

——, 1989. 'The evidence for bone modification by early hominids in southern Africa', in Robson Bonnichsen and Marcella H. Sorg (eds), *Bone Modification*, Centre for the Study of First Americans, University of Maine, Orona, Maine:291–7.

Brain, Charles Kimberlin and Sillen, A., 1988. 'Evidence from the Swartkrans cave for the earliest use of fire', *Nature*, 336:464–6.

Breckwoldt, Roland, 1988. *A Very Elegant Animal: the dingo*, Angus and Robertson, North Ryde, NSW.

Brown, Robert, 1984. *The Nature of Social Laws: Machiavelli to Mill*, Cambridge University Press, Cambridge.

Brugmann, Jeb, 2009. *Welcome to the Urban Revolution: how cities are changing the world*, University of Queensland Press, St Lucia.

Budiansky, Stephen, 2000. *The Truth about Dogs*, Viking Penguin, NY.

Bunney, Sarah, 1990. 'First Australians were earliest seafarers', *New Scientist*, 126:12.

——, 1994. 'Most ancient human came from Afar,' *New Scientist*, 1 October:16.

Burenhult, Göran (gen. ed.), 1993. *The First Humans: human origins and history to 10,000BC*, American Museum of Natural History, Harper Collins, New York.

Cachel, Susan, 1975. 'A new view of speciation in *Australopithecus*', in Russell H. Tuttle (ed.), *Palaeoanthropology: morphology and palaeoecology*, Mouton Publishers, The Hague:183–201.

Caius, Iohannes, 1969 (1576). *Of Englishe Dogges*, (trans. from Latin by Abraham Fleming), Theatrum Orbis Terrarum Ltd, Amsterdam and Da Capo Press, New York.

Calhoun, John B., 1971. 'Space and the strategy of life', in Aristide H. Esser (ed.), *Behavior and Environment: the use of space by animals and man*, Plenum Press, New York:329–87.

Cann, Rebecca L.; Stoneking, Mark and Wilson, Alan C., 1987. 'Mitochondrial DNA and human evolution', *Nature*, 325:31–6.

Chao, Sister M. John Paul, 1989. 'A new sense of community: perspectives from a squatter settlement', in Charmain Thirwall and Philip J. Hughes (eds), *The Ethics of Development: in search of justice,* papers presented at and arising from the 17th Waigani Seminar, University of Papua New Guinea Press, Port Moresby:88–106.

Chesterton, G.K., 1944 (1915). *Wine, Water and Song*, Methuen & Co. Ltd., London.

Churchill, Steven E. and Trinkaus, Erik, 1990. 'Neandertal scapular glenoid morphology,' *American Journal of Physical Anthropology*, 83:147–160.

Clark, J.G.D., 1971. *Excavations at Star Carr: an early mesolithic site at Seamer near Scarborough, Yorkshire*, Cambridge at the University Press, Cambridge.

Clark, Stephen Richard Lyster, 1977. *The Moral Status of Animals*, Clarendon Press, Oxford.

Clark, Wilfred Edward Le Gros, 1959. *The Antecedents of Man: an introduction to the evolution of primates*, Quadrangle Books, New York Times Book Co., NY.

Clark, Graham and Piggott, Stuart, *Prehistoric Societies*, Hutchinson and Co., London.

Clutton-Brock, Juliet, 1984. 'Dog', in Mason, I.L. (ed.), *Evolution of Domestic Animals,* Longman, London:198-211.

——, 1987. *A Natural History of Domesticated Mammals*, British Museum (Natural History) in association with Cambridge University Press, Cambridge.

Cole, Sonia, 1970, *The Neolithic Revolution*, 5th edn, British Museum (Natural History), London.

Coppens, Yves, 1994. 'The East Side story: the origin of humankind', *Scientific American*, May:62–9.

Coppinger, Raymond and Coppinger, Lorna, 2001. *Dogs: a new understanding of canine origin, behavior, and evolution*, University of Chicago Press, Chicago.

Coren, Stanley, 2008. *The Modern Dog: a joyful exploration of how we live with dogs today*, Free Press, NY.

Crocker, D.R., 1984. 'Anthropomorphism: bad practice, honest prejudice?, in Georgina Ferry (ed.), *The Understanding of Animals*, Basil Blackwell, Oxford:304–13.

Crockford, Susan, 2006. *Rhythms of Life: thyroid hormone and the origin of species*, www.trafford.com, Trafford Publishing, Victoria BC, Canada.

Croft, D.B. (ed.), 1991. *Australian People and Animals in Today's Dreamtime: the role of comparative psychology in the management of natural resources*, published for the International Society for Comparative Psychology and University of Calabria by Praeger, New York.

——, 1991. 'The relationship between people and animals: an Australian perspective', in Croft, D.B. (ed.), *Australian People and Animals in Today's Dreamtime: the role of comparative psychology in the management of natural resources*, published for the International Society for Comparative Psychology and University of Calabria by Praeger, New York:1–20.

Cromer, Alan, 1993. *Uncommon Sense: the heretical nature of science*, Oxford University Press, New York and Oxford.

Croxton Smith, A., 1948. 'The dog in history', in Brian Vesey-Fitzgerald (ed.), *The Book of the Dog*, Nicholson and Watson, London.

Csányi, Vilmos, 2000. *If Dogs Could Talk: exploring the canine mind*, Trans. R.E. Quandt, North Point Press, Division of Farrar, Straub and Giroux, NY.

Daniel, Glyn E., 1950. *A Hundred Years of Archaeology*, Gerald Duckworth and Co., London.

Darnton, John, 1996. *Neanderthal: their time has come*, Hutchinson, London.

Darwin, Charles, 1901 (1845). *A Naturalist's Voyage Round the World: journal of researches into the natural history of the countries visited during the voyage round the world of H.M.S. 'Beagle' under command of Captain Fitz Roy, R.N.S.,* 2nd edn, John Murray, London.

——, 1901 (1859). *The Origin of Species, by means of natural selection or the preservation of favoured races in the struggle for life,* Popular Impression, John Murray, London.

——, *1882. The Variation of Animals and Plants under Domestication*, second edition revised, two volumes, John Murray, London.

——, 2004 (1879). *The Descent of Man, and Selection in Relation to Sex*, with introduction by James Moore and Adrian Desmond, Penguin Books, London.

Davidson, Iain and Noble, William, 1990. 'On the evolution of language', *Current Anthropology*, 34(2):165–70.

Davis, Simon J.M., 1987. *The Archeology of Animals*, B.T. Batsford, London.

——, 1991. 'When and why did prehistoric people domesticate animals? Some evidence from Israel and Cyprus,' in Offer Bar-Yosef and Francois R. Valla, *The Natufian Culture in the Levant*, International Monographs in Prehistory, Ann Arbor, Michigan:381–390.

Davis, S.J.M. and Valla, F.R., 1978. 'Evidence for the domestication of the dog 12,000 years ago in the Natufian of Israel', *Nature*, 276:608–10

Dawkins, Richard, 1981. 'In defence of selfish genes', *Philosophy*, 56:556–73.

——, 1982. *The Extended Phenotype: the gene as the unit of selection*, WH Freeman and Company, Oxford and San Francisco.

——, 1986. *The Blind Watchmaker*, Longman Scientific and Technical, Essex, England.

——, 1989. *The Selfish Gene*, new edition, Oxford University Press, Oxford (first published 1976).

——, 1996. *River Out of Eden: a Darwinian view of life*, Phoenix, Orion, London.

——, with Yan Wong, 2004. *The Ancestor's Tale: a pilgrimage to the dawn of life*, Weidenfeld & Nicolson, London.

——, 2006. *The God Delusion*, Bantam Press, London.

Deacon, T.D., 1989. 'The neural circuitry underlying primate calls and human language', *Human Evolution*, 4:367–401.

Degerböl, M., 1961. 'On a find of a preboreal domestic dog (Canis familiaris L.) from Star Carr, Yorkshire, with remarks on other Mesolithic dogs', *Proceedings of the Prehistoric Society*, 27(3):35–55.

Degler, Carl N., 1991. *In Search of Human Nature: the decline and revival of Darwinism in American social thought*, Oxford University Press, New York.

Delius, Juan D., 1989. 'Of mind memes and brain bugs, a natural history of culture', in Walter Koch (ed.), *The Nature of Culture*, proceedings of the International and Interdisciplinary Symposium, October 7–11 1986, in Bochum, Studienverlag Dr. Norbert Brockmeyer, Bochum, Federal Republic of Germany:26–79.

Dennis-Bryan, Kim and Clutton-Brock, Juliet, 1988. *Dogs of the Last Hundred Years at the British Museum*, British Museum (Natural History), London.

Descartes, René, 1949. *A Discourse on Method*, trans. John Veitch, J.M. Dent and Sons, London.

Dodson, Calaway, 1975. 'Coevolution of orchids and bees', in Lawrence E. Gilbert and Peter H. Raven (eds), *Coevolution in Animals and Plants*, University of Texas, Austin:89–99.

Dogan, Mattei and Pahre, Robert, 1990. *Creative Marginality: innovation at the intersections of social sciences*, Westview Press, Boulder, Colorado.

Doolan, Robert, 1996. 'Oh! My aching wisdom teeth!', *Creation*, 18(3): 17 (www.answersingenesis.org/creation/v18/i3/wisdom_teeth.asp).

Doolittle, W. Ford, 1987. 'From selfish gene to Gaia', in John M. Robson (ed.), *Origin and Evolution of the Universe: evidence for design?* McGill-Queens University Press, Kingston and Montreal.

Driscoll Carlos, Macdonald, David W. and O'Brien, Stephen J., 2009. 'From wild animals to domestic pets, an evolutionary view of domestication', *Proceedings National Academy of Sciences*, 106 (supplement 1):9971-9978, June 16.

DuBrul, E. Lloyd, 1958. *Evolution of the Speech Apparatus*, Charles C. Thomas, Springfield, Illinois.

Ducos, Pierre, 1989. 'Defining domestication: a clarification', trans. Marie Matthews, in Juliet Clutton-Brock (ed.), *The Walking Larder: patterns of domestication, pastoralism, and predation*, Unwin Hyam, London:28–30.

Dunbar, Robin, 1996. *Grooming, Gossip, and the Evolution of Language*, Harvard University Press, Cambridge, Massachusetts.

Eiseley, Loren, 1961. *Darwin's Century: evolution and the men who discovered it*, Anchor Books, Doubleday and Company, Garden City, New York.

Emy, Hugh V., 1989. 'From a positive to a cultural science: towards a new rationale for political studies', *Political Studies*, XXXVII:188–204.

Epstein, H., 1971. *The Origin of the Domesticated Animals of Africa*, volume 1, Africana Publishing Corporation, London.

Ferry, Georgina (ed.), 1984. *The Understanding of Animals*, Basil Blackwell, Oxford.

Field, E.J. and Harrison, R.J., 1957. *Anatomical Terms: their origin and derivation*, W. Heffer and Sons, Cambridge.

Fiennes, Richard and Fiennes, Alice, 1968. *The Natural History of the Dog*, Weidenfeld and Nicolson, London.

Finucane, R.C., 1987. 'Witchcraft', in Eliade, Mircea (ed.), *The Encyclopaedia of Religion*, Macmillan Publishing, New York.

Flannery, Timothy Fridtjof, 1993. 'Moving animals from place to place', in Göran Burenhult (gen. ed.), *The First Humans: human origins and history to 10,000 BC*, American Museum of Natural History, Harper Collins Publishers, New York:175.

——, 1995. *The Future Eaters: an ecological history of the Australasian lands and people*, Reed Books, Port Melbourne.

Flint R.F., 1989. 'Pleistocene Epoch', in *The New Encyclopaedia Britannica*, Goetz P.W. (ed.), vol. 19, Britannica, Chicago.

Forester, C.S., 1968. *Hornblower and the Hotspur*, Penguin Books, Middlesex, England.

Fox, Michael W., 1974. *Concepts in Ethology: animal and human behavior*, University of Minnesota Press, Minneapolis.

——, 1975. 'Pet – owner relations', in R.S. Anderson (ed.), *Pet Animals and Society*, British Small Animal Veterinary Association, Baillière Tindall, London:37–53.

——, 1978. *The Dog: its domestication and behavior*, Garland STPM Press, New York.

——, 1978. 'Man, wolf, and dog', in Roberta L. Hall and Henry S. Sharp (eds), *Wolf and Man: evolution in parallel*, Academic Press, New York:19–30.

——, 1980. *Returning to Eden: animal rights and human responsibility*, Viking Press, New York.

Fuller, J.L. and DuBuis, E.M., 1962. 'The behaviour of dogs', in E.S.E. Hafez (ed.), *The Behaviour of Domestic Animals*, Baillière, Tindall and Cox, London:415–52.

Gagnon, Sylvain and Dorè, Francois Y., 1993. 'Search behavior of dogs *(Canis familiaris)'*, *Animal Learning and Behavior*, 21(3):246–54.

Galton, Francis, 1907. *Inquiries into Human Faculty and Its Development*, J.M. Dent and Sons, London (Second Edition).

Gamble, Clive, 1995. *Timewalkers: the prehistory of global colonization*, Penguin Books, London.

Germonpré, Mietje; Sablin, Mikhail V.; Stevens, Rhiannon E.; Hedges, Robert E.M.; Hofreiter, Michael; Stiller, Mathias and Jaenicke-Desprese, Viviane, 2008. 'Feral dogs and wolves from Paleolithic sites in Belgium, the Ukraine and Russia: oesteometry, ancient DNA and stable isotopes', *Journal of Archaeological Science*, accepted manuscript 26 September.

Gore, Rick; Garrett, Kenneth and Schlecht, Richard, 1996. 'The dawn of humans: Neandertals', *National Geographic*, 189(1):2–35.

Gould, Stephen Jay, 1980. 'Is a new and general theory of evolution emerging?', *Palaeobiology*, 6(1):119–30.

——, 1985. 'The paradox of the first tier: an agenda for palaeobiology', *Palaeobiology*, 11(1):2–12.

——, 1986. *Ever Since Darwin: reflections in natural history*, Penguin Books, Middlesex.

Gould, Stephen Jay and Vrba, Elizabeth S., 1982. 'Exaptation – a missing term in the science of form', *Palaeobiology*, 8(1):4–15.

Groves, Colin P., 1989. 'Natural selection and intelligent ancestors', *Mankind*, Anthropological Society of NSW, 19(1):76–82.

——, 1993. *The Domestication of Animals*, videotape held at Chifley Library, Australian National University.

——, 1994. 'The origin of modern humans', *Interdisciplinary Science Reviews*, 19(1):23–34.

——, 1998. In David Paterson's film *The Secret Life of the Dog*, Boa Picture Company production for Channel 4 in association with Discovery Channel, Channel 4 Television Corporation.

——, 1999. 'The advantages and disadvantages of being domesticated', *Perspectives on Human Biology*, 4 (1), 1-12 (A Keynote Address).

Haas, G., 1966. *On the Vertebrate Fauna of the Lower Pleistocene Site 'Ubeidiya*, The Israeli Academy of Sciences and Humanities, Jerusalem.

Hall, Roberta L., 1978. 'Variability and speciation in canids and hominids', in Roberta L. Hall and Henry S. Sharp (eds), *Wolf and Man: evolution in parallel*, Academic Press, New York:153–77.

Hamilton, Annette, 1971–1972. ‘Aboriginal man’s best friend?’, *Mankind*, Anthropological Society of NSW, 8(4):287–95.

Hayden, B., 1975–1976. ‘Dingoes: pets or producers?’, *Mankind*, Anthropological Society of NSW, 10(1)11–15.

Haynes, Robert H., 1987. ‘The “purpose” of chance in light of the physical basis of evolution’, in John M. Robson (ed.). *Origin and Evolution of the Universe: evidence for design?*, McGill-Queen’s University Press, Kingston and Montreal:1–31.

Hemmer, Helmut, 1990. *Domestication: the decline of environmental appreciation*, (trans. Neil Beckhaus), Cambridge University Press, Cambridge.

Henry, Donald O., 1989. *From Foraging to Agriculture: the Levant at the end of the Ice Age*, University of Pennsylvania Press, Philadelphia.

Horwitz, L. Kolska, 1990. ‘The origin of partially digested bones recovered from archeological contexts in Israel’, *Paléorient*, 16(1):97–107.

Houpt, Katherine A. and Woslki, Thomas R., 1982. *Domestic Animal Behavior for Veterinarians and Animal Scientists*, Iowa State University Press, Ames.

Huot, Jean-Louis, 1978. ‘The man–faced bull L.76.17 of Larsa’, *Sumer*, XXXIV(1–2):104–10.

Hyams, Edward, 1972. *Animals in the Service of Man: 10000 years of domestication*, J.M. Dent and Sons, London.

Jelinek, Arthur J., 1994. 'Hominids, energy, environment, and behaviour in the Late Pleistocene', in Matthew H. Nitecki and Doris V. Nitecki (eds), *Origins of Anatomically Modern Humans*, Plenum Press, New York:67–92.

Jhala, Yadvendradev and Sharma, Dinesh Kumar, 2004. 'The ancient wolves of India,' *International Wolf* (www.wolf.org), Summer: 15–16.

Jolly, Clifford and Plogg, Fred, 1987. *Physical Anthropology and Archaeology*, McGraw-Hill, NY.

Jones, Steve, 1994. *The Language of the Genes: biology, history and the evolutionary future*, Flamingo (Harper Collins), London.

Kennedy, Wardlaw, 1899. *Beasts: thumb-nail studies in pets*, Macmillan Co., London.

Kimbel, William H., Johanson, Donald C. and Rak, Yoel, 1994. 'The first skull and other new discoveries of *Australopithecus afarensis* at Hadar, Ethiopia', *Nature*, 368:449–51.

King, D. Brett and Viney, Wayne, 1992. 'Modern history of pragmatic and sentimental attitudes towards animals and the selling of comparative psychology', *Journal of Comparative Psychology*, 106(2):190–5.

Klein, Richard G., 1994. 'The problem of modern human origins', in Matthew H. Nitecki and Doris V. Nitecki (eds), *Origins of Anatomically Modern Humans*, Plenum Press, New York:3–17.

Klieman, Devra, 1967. 'Some aspects of social behavior in the *Canidae*', *American Zoologist*, 7:365–72.

Knapp, Caroline, 1999. *Pack of Two: the intricate bond between people and dogs*, Anchor, Sydney.

Koch, Walter A. (ed.), 1989. *The Nature of Culture*, proceedings of the International and Interdisciplinary Symposium, October 7-11, 1986 in Bochum, Studienverlag Dr. Norbert Brockmeyer, Bochum, Federal Republic of Germany.

Koler-Matznick, Janice, 2002. 'The Origin of the Dog Revisited,' *Anthrozoös,* 15(2), 98-117.

Kolig, Erich, 1973–1974. 'Aboriginal man's best foe?', *Mankind*, Anthropological Society of NSW, 9(2):122–3.

Kropotkin, Petr, 1939 (1914). *Mutual Aid: a factor in evolution*, Penguin Books, Middlesex.

Laird, Marshall, 1984. 'Overview and perspectives', in Marshall Laird (ed.), *Commerce and the Spread of Pests and Disease Vectors*, Praeger Publishing, New York.

Laitman, Jeffrey T., 1990. 'The anatomy of human speech', *Natural History*, 93(8):20–7.

Landes, David, 1999. *The Wealth and Poverty of Nations: why some are so rich and some so poor*, Abacus Books, Little, Brown and Company (UK), London.

Lanpo, Jia, 1980. *Early Man in China*, Foreign Languages Press, Beijing.

Larrick, Roy and Ciochon, Russell L., 1996. 'The African emergence and early Asian dispersals of the genus *Homo*,' *American Scientist*, November – December.

Lawrence, Elizabeth Atwood, 2000. 'A case for a naturalistic perspective: response to Paxton', *Anthrozoös*, 13(1):9–10.

Lawton, Graham, 2009. 'Uprooting Darwin's tree', *New Scientist*, 24 January: 34–39.

Leakey, Richard E., 1981. *The Making of Mankind*, Michael Joseph Limited, London.

——, 1994. *The Origin of Humankind*, Science Masters in association with Basic Books, Harper Collins, New York.

Leakey, Richard E. and Lewin, Roger, 1982. *Origins: what new discoveries reveal about the emergence of our species and its possible future*, Futura, Macdonald and Co., London.

Leeds, Anthony and Vayda, Andrew P., 1965. *Man, Culture and Animals: the role of animals in human ecological adjustments*, Publication 78, American Association for the Advancement of Science, Washington DC.

Leslie, John, 1978. 'God and scientific verifiability', *Philosophy*, 53:71–9.

Lewinsohn, Richard, 1954. *Animals Men and Myths: a history of the influence of animals on civilization and culture*, Victor Gollanz, London.

Leyhausen, Paul, 1989. 'The evolution of cultural dimensions', in Walter Koch (ed.), *The Nature of Culture*, proceedings of the International and Interdisciplinary Symposium, October 7-11, 1986 in Bochum, Studienverlag Dr Norbert Brockmeyer, Bochum, Federal Republic of Germany:4–25.

Lieberman, Philip, 1984. *The Biology and Evolution of Language*, Harvard University Press, Cambridge, Massachusetts.

Lindsay, Steven R., 2005. *Handbook of Applied Dog Behavior and Training* (3 vols), Iowa State University Press, Ames Iowa: Blackwell.

Little, John, 2006. *Christine's Ark: biography of Christine Townend*, Pan Macmillan, Sydney.

Livingstone, Frank B., 1992. 'Gene flow in the Pleistocene', *Human Biology*, 64(1):67–80.

London, Jack, 1983 (1903). *The Call of the Wild*, Octopus Books, London.

——, 1983 (1906). *White Fang*, Octopus Books, London.

——, 1904. *The Sea-Wolf*, The Macmillan Company, New York.

Lorenz, Konrad Z., 1952. *King Solomon's Ring: new light on animal ways*, Methuen and Co., London.

——, 1959. *Man Meets Dog*, Pan Books, London (first published 1954 by Methuen and Co.).

——, 1968. *On Aggression*, University Paperback, Norfolk, England.

Lumholz, C., 1980 (1888). *Among Cannibals*, The Australian National University Press, Canberra.

Lynch, James J. and McCarthy, John F., 1969. 'Social responding in dogs: heart rate changes to a person', *Psychophysiology*, 5(4):389–98.

Lynch, James J.; Fregin, G. Frederick; Mackie, James B. and Monroe, Russell R., 1974. 'Heart rate changes in the horse to human contact', *Psychophysiology*, 11(4):472–78.

Mackie, J.L., 1978. 'The Law of the Jungle: moral alternatives and the principles of evolution', *Philosophy*, 53:455–64.

Marchant, R.A., 1962. *Beasts of Fact and Fable*, Phoenix House, London.

Mason, I.L. (ed.), 1984. *Evolution of Domestic Animals*, Longman, London.

Matthews, Gareth B., 1978. 'Animals and the unity of psychology', Philosophy, 53:437–54.

MacCallum Research and Mackay, Hugh, 1992. *What Australians Feel about their Pets: a study of our attitudes to cat and dog ownership; motivations and benefits of ownership: the personal, familial and social context*, Petcare Information and Advisory Service, West Melbourne.

MacNeilage, Peter F., 2008. *The Origin of Speech*, Oxford University Press, New York.

McAllister, Peter., 2009. *Manthropology: the science of the inadequate modern male*, Hachette Australia, Sydney.

McBride, Glenorchy, 1991. 'Relationships between people and animals', in Croft, D.B. (ed.), *Australian People and Animals in Today's Dreamtime: the role of comparative psychology in the management of natural resources*, published for International Society for Comparative Psychology and University of Calabria by Praeger, New York.:93-105.

McFadden, Johnjoe, 2000. *Quantum Evolution: life in the multiverse*, Flamingo, London.

McGuire, Bill, 2002. *A Guide to the End of the World: everything you never wanted to know*, Oxford University Press, Oxford and New York.

McKie, Robin, 2000. *ape•man: the story of human evolution*, BBC Worldwide, London.

Mech, L. David, 1970. *The Wolf: the ecology and behavior of an endangered species*, published for the American Museum of Natural History, Natural History Press, New York.

Menzel, Rudolph and Menzel, Rudolphina, 1948. 'Observations on the pariah dog', in Brian Vesey-Fitzgerald (ed.), *The Book of the Dog*, Nicholson and Watson, London:968–90.

Messent, Peter, 1983. *Understanding your dog: the intelligent person's guide to a lifelong relationship with another species*, Stein and Day, New York.

——, 1987. 'Problems with an encompassing theory', *Anthrozoös*, 1(3):149–50.

Mestel, Rosie, 1993. 'Barking dogs are stuck in adolescence', *New Scientist*, February, 27:9.

Midgley, Mary, 1978. *Beast and Man*, Harvester Press, Sussex.

——, 1978. 'The objection to systematic humbug', *Philosophy*, 53:147–69.

——, 1979. 'Gene-juggling', *Philosophy*, 54:439–58.

Miklósi, Ádám, 2005. 'Dog – human relationship in an evolutionary perspective', abstract, 12 July (Eötvös Lorand University).

Miles, David, 1978. *An Introduction to Archaeology*, Ward Lock, London.

Miller, Susan, 1993. Correspondence, *Anthrozoös*, 6(3):146–7.

Milstein, Mati, 2008. 'Neandertals had big mouths, gaped widely', *National Geographic News*, 2 May, webpage.

Morell, Virginia, 1997. 'The origin of dogs: running with the wolves', Research News (Evolutionary Biology), *Science*, June 13, 276:1647–8.

Morey, Darcy, 2006. 'Burying key evidence: the social bond between dogs and people', *Journal of Archaeological Science*, 33:158 – 175.

Morey, Darcy F. and Wiant, Michael D., 1992. 'Early Holocene domestic dog burials from the North American Midwest', *Current Anthropology*, 33(2):224–9.

Morris, C., 1900. *Man and His Ancestors*, Macmillan, New York.

Morris, Desmond, 1967. *The Naked Ape*, Corgi Books, Transworld Publishers, London.

——, 1986. *Dog Watching*, Jonathan Cape, London.

——, 1994. *The Human Animal: a personal view of the human species*, BBC Books, London.

Morrison, Reg, 2003. *Plague Species: is it in our genes?*, Reed New Holland, Sydney.

Mowat, Farley, 1979. *Never Cry Wolf*, Pan Books, London.

Murray, Richard W. and Penridge, Helen, 1997. *Dogs and Cats in the Urban Environment: a handbook of municipal pet management*, second edition, Chiron Media, Mooloolah, Queensland.

Nath, B., 1973. 'Prehistoric fauna excavated from various sites in India with special reference to domestication', in János Matolcsi (ed.), *Domeskitations forschung und Geschichte der Haustíere*, Kiado, Budapest.

Newby, Jonica, 1997. *The Pact for Survival: humans and their animal companions*, Australian Broadcasting Corporation, Sydney (also released as *Animal Attraction*).

Nitecki, Matthew H. and Nitecki, Doris V. (eds), *Origins of Anatomically Modern Humans,* Plenum Press, New York and London.

Noske, Barbara, 1989. *Humans and Other Animals: beyond the boundaries of anthropology*, Pluto Press, London.

Notes from field studies, 1993/4. Jaipur, Cochin, Pondicherry, Madras, New Delhi and Bangkok.

Notes from field studies, 1994. Merrimans Local Aboriginal Land Council, Wallaga Koori Village, NSW.

O'Brian, Patrick, 2010. *The Final Unfinished Voyage of Jack Aubrey*, Harper Collins, London.

O'Brien, Eileen, 1984. 'What was the Acheulian hand ax?', *Natural History*, 93(7): 20-23, July. American Museum of Natural History, NY.

O'Brien, Peter H., 1991. 'The introduced wild and feral mammals of Australia: past and present relationships with humans as determinants of their status', in D.B. Croft (ed.), *Australian People and Animals in Today's Dreamtime: the role of comparative psychology in the management of natural resources*, published for the International Society for Comparative Psychology and University of Calabria by Praeger, New York:71–92.

Owen, James, 2004. 'Neandertals beaten by rivals' word skills,' *National Geographic News*, 24 November.

——, 2005. 'Neandertals had long childhood, tooth study suggests,' *National Geographic News*, 20 September.

Palmer, Arthur Beau, 1985. 'Report on contemporary tradition and neo-traditional Aboriginal man-canine relationships', Aboriginal and Torres Strait Islander Commission, Woden, ACT.

Pang, Jun-Feng; Kluetsch, Cornelya; Zou, Xiao-Ju; Zhang, Ai-bing; Luo, Li-yang; Angleby, Helen; Ardalan, Arman; Ekström, Camilla; Sköllermo, Anna; Lundeberg, Joakim; Matsumura, Shuichi; Leitner, Thomas; Zhang, Ya-ping; and Savolainen, Peter, 2009. 'mtDNA indicates a single origin of dogs south of Yangtze River, less than 16,300 years ago, from numerous wolves', MBE Advanced Access: 1 September.

Passmore, J., 1974. *Man's Responsibility for Nature*, Duckworth, London.

Paul Shepard and Daniel McKinley (eds), 1969. *The Subversive Science: essays toward an ecology of man*, Houghton Miflin, Boston.

Paterson, David 1998. *The Secret Life of the Dog*, Boa Picture Company production for Channel 4 in association with Discovery Channel, Channel 4 Television Corporation.

Paxton, David W., 1994. 'Community involvement and urban dogs – some ideas', in D.W. Paxton (ed.), *Urban Animal Management: proceedings of the third national conference on urban animal management in Australia,*

Canberra, 1994, Australian Veterinary Association, Artarmon, NSW:103–12.
——, 2000. 'A case for a naturalistic perspective', *Anthrozoös*, 13(1): 5–7, 13–14, with comments by Elizabeth Atwood Lawrence and Marc Bekoff.
Pearce, Jonathan, c1993. 'The street dogs of India', *The Animals' Voice Magazine*, 7 (2): 21–4 (World Society for the Protection of Animals).
Perkins, Dexter, 1973. 'A critique of methods of quantifying faunal remains from archaeological sites', in János Matolcsi (ed.), *Domeskitations forschung und Geschichte der Haustíere*, Kiadõ, Budapest:367–9.
Pinker, Steven, 1994. *The Language Instinct: how the mind creates language*, William Morrow and Company, New York.
Protsch, Reiner and Berger, Rainer, 1973. 'Earliest radiocarbon dates for domesticated animals', *Science*, 179:235–9.
Rachels, James, 1991. *Created from Animals: the moral implications of Darwinism*, Oxford University Press, Oxford.
Rak, Yoel, 1986. 'The Neandertal: a new look at an old face', *Journal of Human Evolution*, 15(2): 151–164.
Rautenbach, G.H., Boomker, J. and De Villiers, I.L., 1991. 'A descriptive study of the canine population in a rural town in southern Africa', *Journal of the South African Veterinary Association*, 62(4):158–62.
Reeve, Rod, 2007. *Hot-Spotting: an Australian delivering foreign aid*, Wakefield Press, Kent Town, South Australia.

Regan, Tom, 1989. 'Ill-gotten gains', in Langley, Gill (ed.), *Animal Experimentation: the consensus changes*, Macmillan Press, Hampshire and London:19–41.

Rensberger, Boyce, 1981. 'Facing the past', *Science 81*, October, American Association for the Advancement of Science:40–51.

Ritvo, Harriet, 1987. *The Animal Estate: the English and other creatures in the Victorian age*, Harvard University Press, Cambridge.

Rogers, Lesley J. and Kaplan, Gisela, 2003. *Spirit of the Wild Dog: the world of wolves, coyotes, jackals & dingoes*, Allen & Unwin, Sydney.

Rose, Mark, 1997. 'Neandertal DNA', *Archaeology*, 50(5), September October.

Rostow, W.W., 1975. *How It All Began: origins of the modern economy*, Methuen, London.

Rowan, A.N. (ed.), 1986. 'Dog aggression and the Pit Bull Terrier', proceedings (plus additional material) of a workshop organised by the Tufts Center for Animals on 17 July, Tufts University School of Veterinary Medicine, Maryland.

——, 1994. 'Research quality, journal publication, and academic discourse', *Anthrozoös*, 7(1):2–3.

——, 1994. 'The health benefits of human–animal interactions', *Anthrozoös*, 7(2):85–9.

Rowley-Conwy, Peter, 1993. 'Genes, languages and archaeology', in Göran Burenhult (gen. ed.), *The First Humans: human origins and history to 10,000BC*, American Museum of Natural History, Harper Collins, New York.

Rudgley, Richard, 1999. *Lost Civilizations of the Stone Age*, Arrow Books, London.

Runciman, W.G., 1989. *Confessions of a Reluctant Theorist: selected essays*, Harvester Wheatsheaf, New York.

Ryder, Richard D., 1989. *Animal Revolution: changing attitudes to speciesism*, Basil Blackwell, Oxford.

Schleidt, Wolfgang M., 1990. 'Biological bases of age specific behaviour: the companions in man's world', *Essays in Memoriam of Konrad Lorenz*, International Symposium on Evolutionary Aspects of Behavioural Sciences May 29, University of Gothenburg, Sweden.

Schleidt, Wolfgang and Shalter, Michael D., 2003. 'Co-evolution of humans and canids: an alternative view of dog domestication: Homo Homini Lupus?', *Evolution and Cognition*, 9(1):57–72.

Scott, John Paul, 1967. 'The evolution of social behavior in dogs and wolves', *American Zoologist*, 7:373–81.

——, 1972. *Animal Behavior*, 2nd edn revised, University of Chicago Press, Chicago.

Scott Elliott, G.F., 1915. *Prehistoric man and his story*, Seeley, Service and Company.

Serpell, James A., 1986. *In the Company of Animals: a study of human-animal relationships*, Basil Blackwell, Oxford.

——, 1987. 'In defence of ethology', *Anthrozoös*, 1(3):145–6.

——, 1991. 'Beneficial effects of pet ownership on some aspects of human health and behaviour', *Journal of the Royal Society of Medicine*, 84:717–20.

Sharma, Dinesh Kumar; Maldonado, Jesus E.; Jhala, Yadrendradev V.; and Fleischer, Robert C., 2004. 'Ancient wolf lineages in India', *Proceedings of the Royal Society Biology Letters* (Supplement), 271: S1-S4.

Sharp, Henry S., 1978. 'Comparative ethnology of the wolf and the Chipewyan', in Roberta L. Hall and Henry S. Sharp (eds), *Wolf and Man: evolution in parallel*, Academic Press, New York:55–79.

Sheldrake, Rupert, 1994 (1988). *The Presence of the Past: morphic resonance and the habits of nature*, HarperCollins, London.

——, 1999. *Dogs that Know when their Owners are Coming Home:and other unexplained powers of animals*, Hutchinson, London.

Shepard, Paul, 1973. *The Tender Carnivore and the Sacred Game*, Charles Scribner's Sons, New York.

Shipman, Pat, 1984. 'Scavenger hunt', *Natural History*, 93(4):20–27, April, American Museum of Natural History, NY.

Shreeve, James, 1996. *The Neandertal Enigma:solving the mystery of human origins*, Viking, Great Britain.

Silverberg, Robert, 1967. *The Morning of Mankind: prehistoric man in Europe*, World's Work, Great Britain.

Sisson, Septimus, 1953 (1910). *The Anatomy of the Domestic Animals*, revised by James Daniel Grossman, W.B. Saunders Company, Philadelphia.

Slurink, P., 1993. 'Ecological dominance and the final sprint in hominid evolution', *Human Evolution*, 8(4):265–73.

Smith, V.L., 1977. 'The primitive hunter culture, Pleistocene extinction, and the rise of agriculture', in Smith, V.L. (ed.), *Economics of Natural and Environmental Resources*, Gordon and Breach, New York.

Stanley, Steven M., 1992. 'An ecological theory for the evolution of *Homo*', *Paleobiology*, 18(3):237–57.

Stevenson, Marc, 1978. 'Dire Wolf systematics and behavior', in Roberta L. Hall and Henry S. Sharp (eds), *Wolf and Man: evolution in parallel*, Academic Press, New York:179–96.

Street, Philip, 1975. *Animal Partners and Parasites*, David & Charles, Great Britain.

Stringer, Christopher B., 1994. 'Out of Africa: a personal history', in Matthew H. Nitecki and Doris V. Nitecki (eds), *Origins of Anatomically Modern Humans*, Plenum Press, New York and London:149–72.

Stringer, Christopher B. and McKie, Robin, 1996. *African Exodus: the origins of modern humanity*, Jonathan Cape, London.

Stringer, Christopher B. and Andrews, Peter, 2005. *The Complete World of Human Evolution*, Thames and Hudson, London.

Süskind, Patrick, 1987. *Perfume: the story of a murderer*, (transl. John E. Woods), Penguin Books, London.

Svoboda, Elizabeth, 2006. 'Neandertal gene study reveals early split with humans,' *National Geographic News*, 26 October.

Tangri, D. and Wyncoll, G., 1989. 'Of mice and men: is the presence of commensal animals in archaeological sites a positive correlate of sedentism?', *Paléorient*, 15(2):85–94.

Templeton, Alan R., 2002. 'Out of Africa again and again', *Nature*, 416: 45– 61.

Thomas, Elizabeth Marshall, 1994. *The Hidden Life of Dogs*, Weidenfeld and Nicolson, London.

Thomas, Keith, 1983. *Man and the Natural World: changing attitudes in England 1500-1800*, Allen Lane, London.

Thompson, D'Arcy Wentworth, 1949. *The Works of Aristotle Translated into English, IV, Historia Animalium*, Oxford University Press, Oxford (first published in 1910).

Thomson, J.A.K., 1955. *The Ethics of Aristotle: the Nicomachean Ethics*, Penguin Books, Middlesex.

Trinkaus, E. and Shipman, P., 1993. *The Neandertals: changing the image of mankind*, Alfred A. Knopf, New York.

Trut, Liudmilla, 1998. In David Paterson's film *The Secret Life of the Dog*, Boa Picture Company production for Channel 4 in association with Discovery Channel, Channel 4 Television Corporation.

Turner, Alan, 1992. 'Large carnivores and earliest European hominids: changing determinants of resource availability during the lower and Middle Pleistocene", *Journal of Human Evolution*, 22: 109–126.

Vesey-Fitzgerald, Brian (ed.), 1948. *The Book of the Dog*, Nicholson and Watson, London.

——, 1957. *The Domestic Dog: an introduction to its history*, Routledge and Keagan Paul, London.

Viegas, Jennifer, 2008. 'First known dog ate big game', *Discovery News*, 17 October, http://dsc.discovery.com/news/2008/10/17/paeolithic-dog-skull.html.

Vilà, Carles; Savolainen, Peter; Maldonado, Jesús E.; Amorim, Isabel R.; Rice, John E.; Honeycutt, Rodney L.; Crandall, Keith A.; Lundeberg, Joakim and Wayne, Robert, 1997. 'Multiple and ancient origins of the domestic dog', *Science*, 276:1687–89.

Waddle, Diane M., 1994. 'Matrix correlation tests support a single origin for modern humans', *Nature*, 368:452–4.

Wahida, Ghanim, 1981. 'The re-excavation of Zarzi, 1971', *Proceedings of the Prehistoric Society*, 47:19–40 (Appendix 3).

Walens, Stanley, 1987. 'Animals', in Mircea Eliade (ed. in chief), *The Encyclopaedia of Religion*, Macmillan, New York, 1:291–6.

Walker, Alan and Shipman, Pat, 1997. *The Wisdom of Bones: in search of human origins*, Phoenix Orion Books, London.

Walters, Ian, 1984. 'Gone to the dogs: a study of bone attrition at a central Australian campsite', *Mankind*, Anthropological Society of NSW, 14(5):389–400.

Wapnish, Paula and Hesse, Brian, 1993. 'Pampered pooches or plain pariahs? The Ashkelon dog burials', *Biblical Archaeologist*, 56 (2): 55–80.

Watch Tower, 1992. *Does God Really Care About Us? If So, Why Does He Permit Suffering? Will It Ever End?*, Bible and Tract Society of Pennsylvania, New York.

Wells, Spencer, 2002. *The Journey of Man: a genetic odyssey*, Princeton University Press, Princeton and Oxford.

White, Isobel M., 1971–1972. 'Hunting dogs at Yalata', *Mankind*, Anthropological Society of NSW, 8(3):201–5.

Wilkinson, Paul F., 1972. 'Oomingmak, a model for man-animal relationships in pre-history', *Current Anthropology*, 13(1):23–44.

Williams, Peter L. and Warwick, Roger (eds), 1980. *Gray's Anatomy*, 36th edn, WB Saunders Company, Philadelphia.

Wills, Christopher, 1995. *The Runaway Brain: the evolution of human uniqueness*, Flamingo, HarperCollins Publishers, London.

Wilson, Edward O., 1975. *Sociobiology: the new synthesis*, Harvard University Press, Cambridge.

——, 1978. *On Human Nature*, Harvard University Press, Cambridge.

——, 1984. 'Sociobiology: a new basis for human nature', in Georgina Ferry (ed.), *The Understanding of Animals*, Basil Blackwell, Oxford:212–18.

——, 1999. *Consilience: the unity of knowledge*, Abacus Little, Brown and Company, London.

Wong, Kate, 2010. 'Neandertal genome study reveals we have a little caveman in us', *Scientific American*, May 6:68.

Wood, H.G., 1920. 'Dogs', in James Hastings et al. (eds), *A Dictionary of Christ and the Gospels*, T. and T. Clark, Edinburgh and Charles Scribner's Sons, New York, 1:64–9.

Yalden-Thompson, D.C., 1978. 'Hume's view of "is – ought" ', *Philosophy*, 53:89–91.

Zeuner, Frederick E., 1963. *A History of Domesticated Animals*, Harper and Rowe, New York.

Index